The View from the Stands

The View from the Stands

◆

A Season with America's Baseball Fans

Johanna Wagner

iUniverse, Inc.
New York Lincoln Shanghai

The View from the Stands
A Season with America's Baseball Fans

iUniverse books may be ordered through booksellers or by contacting:

iUniverse
2021 Pine Lake Road, Suite 100
Lincoln, NE 68512
www.iuniverse.com
1-800-Authors (1-800-288-4677)

ISBN: 0-595-33481-4 (pbk)
ISBN: 0-595-66950-6 (cloth)

Printed in the United States of America

For my family and my heroes,
be they perfect or not.

"You Gotta Believe..."

—*Tug McGraw*

Contents

Preface xi

CHAPTER 1 If You Build It, They Will Come. 1

CHAPTER 2 Circling the Bases: Part 1 14

    Devil Rays. 15

    Marlins 18

    Braves 23

    Rockies 27

    Mets 29

    Yankees. 32

CHAPTER 3 Sluggers, Gloves, and Good Eyes. 35

CHAPTER 4 Circling the Bases: Part II 46

    Blue Jays. 46

    Tigers 50

    Indians 53

    Padres 56

    Dodgers 59

    Giants. 62

    A's. 68

    Angels 71

    Diamondbacks 73

CHAPTER 5 From a Game to a Business 76

CHAPTER 6 Circling the Bases: Part III. 92

    Expos 94

Cardinals 99

Royals 104

Phillies 107

White Sox 111

Brewers 114

Cubs 116

Twins 117

CHAPTER 7   Connections and Community 120

CHAPTER 8   Circling the Bases: Heading for Home 131

Mariners 131

Orioles 134

Astros 136

Rangers 138

Pirates 141

Red Sox 143

Reds 146

CHAPTER 9   Winning the Game 151

Notes 159

Preface

Contraction. That's what started it. Major League Baseball had announced plans to reduce the number of franchises by contracting two teams. Since September 11, I had begun thinking about all the things I had always wanted to do that I had put off. I had always wanted to see all the Major League Baseball stadiums, and now seemed like the time to do it—before two of the existing franchises were gone.

So I started the planning process, at the same time trying to muster up the courage to do all of this traveling alone. As a woman, I was intimidated by the idea of traveling to so many cities and sitting alone at so many baseball games. Despite my initial trepidation, I soon realized this would not only allow me to see the different parks, it would also provide me with the opportunity to visit the different cities and get to know the country.

I wanted to know why some baseball teams could be contracted and what made those teams untenable. Were those towns unfit for baseball? The Twins had a long baseball history and had even won some championships in recent years. How could MLB think of contracting them, and what would Minnesota fans do? Is it really true that baseball could never work in Montreal, or anywhere in Canada for that matter? Why have the Toronto Blue Jays done so well but not the Expos? And why is baseball so popular in St. Louis, while in Kansas City it can't consistently draw a crowd?

I had worked in theater production for twelve years. It seemed to me that I had learned more in that time about nurturing an audience than MLB had in the one hundred years of its existence. With all the talk about baseball being a business, it seemed from the outside that baseball had given little thought to drawing and maintaining its customers. If MLB could eliminate a team like the Twins, how could their business minds claim to understand what we, the fans, wanted from the game?

I felt I could discover what was missing, first by breaking down what it means to be a fan, and then by looking at my stadium experiences. Baseball holds a unique position in the hearts of sports fans. Its history is tied to our history, both personal and national. Though I loved the game before, I now understand it more thoroughly than ever. Its problems are intrinsic to any business, but they can be rectified. Though my study is in no way scientific, I hope it will provide MLB with a better understanding of what we are really looking for when we buy that ticket, and why we care about someone else's business. I examined the different aspects of the game that the average fan comes into contact with, and how every decision a club makes has an effect on the overall fan experience. Some problems, like those concerning stadiums, cannot be rectified easily or at all, but others can be solved with relatively little cost, resulting in better, more knowledgeable fans.

What follows is a reflection on my experiences as a baseball fan, drawn from my childhood, my summer travels, stories from other baseball fans, and books on the sport. It was a journey that allowed me to examine how the fan is treated in each ballpark, and to examine the fan's role in the business of the game. The summer of 2002 was an exciting one to talk to fans, and it was a hard summer to be one.

1

If You Build It, They Will Come...

I don't remember the first moment when baseball became a part of my world. I know that my nanny, Mary Hope (Aunt Mary to me), loved the Reds. They were always on the television while we played cards or I played with my Barbies. I also loved playing ball at recess and during gym. I was a second baseman, and although I secretly hoped the ball would never come to me, I wasn't too bad of a fielder, and I could also bat pretty well. Actually, I could bat very well, and I was great at moving the runner along. My problem was that I "threw like a girl," as Marcus Thermes repeatedly complained. In those days, girls weren't really encouraged to play ball. I'm not sure anyone even realized that they could teach me not to "throw like a girl." Tired of the taunts, I grew content to sit on the bench and fill the role of pinch hitter. Eventually, as the boys became stronger and more coordinated, I stopped playing altogether. (It might be that they simply stopped inviting me to play, but I choose to remember it differently.) I'm not sure to what extent playing the game was responsible for my love of it, but many fans can indeed trace their adoration of the sport back to America's playgrounds.

Aunt Mary was a big fan and took me to a lot of games. Unlike the Cubs fan I met in St. Louis, who remembered precisely that his first game featured Bob Gibson versus Fergie Jenkins and that Ron Santo hit a two-run shot to win the game, I can't recall any specific moments of my early days as a fan. I do remember how I felt as I walked into Riverfront, as well as the city's pride at having arguably the best starting eight ever assembled.

I loved the Reds, although that was an easy thing to do at the time. I have met a lot of folks my age who fell in love with the Reds because of their outstanding play throughout the seventies, and many of those fans lived nowhere near the Ohio Valley. I will never forget how all of their double plays started in the glove of Dave Concepcion and ended in the glove of Tony Perez. Their precision was miraculous to me, especially since I could barely throw from second to first. I remember Pete Rose standing on second—and first and third—dusting himself off after sliding into each base and smiling while picking the skin off his elbows. As a child, I wasn't used to seeing grown men that happy.

I attended playoff games in those early years, and probably a World Series game—unfortunately, I have no way of knowing for sure—and I remember the stadium going wild, with confetti flying and tears flowing throughout the stands. People were screaming, and adults who would normally have been telling me to "quiet down" were jumping for joy. That communal feeling of elation brought on by the Reds' victory sealed my fate as a baseball fan and created a longing in me that would draw me back to baseball time and time again.

As a seven-year-old, I thought that the other teams were just there to play my Reds, so I learned little about them. Although there was the occasional local who liked the Pirates, I'm not sure it occurred to me that there were actually *fans* of other teams. Every now and then, Aunt Mary would stop whatever she was doing in the kitchen to come into the living room and watch Vida Blue or Frank Robinson. Though I knew they were more than just names, they played for other teams, so their feats couldn't possibly compare to those of Bench, Morgan, and Foster.

As I grew up, Aunt Mary was around less and less—she moved out of the house when I was six—and my exposure to professional baseball likewise decreased. However, I still managed to see three to six games a year. The Reds would give free tickets to kids who got As on their report cards, so I tried to be a model student. However, even if I did have tickets, it was hard at times to find someone to take me. I often went with Paula Ling's family. Paula and her sister were straight-A students and would often share their tickets with me. Despite the fact that baseball made me work harder in school, I often hear stories about people in New York leaving school in the middle of the day to sneak off to Ebbets Field and watch the great Brooklyn Dodgers of the 1950s. There aren't many day games during the week anymore. There aren't many free tickets either.

Though I think I attended a game in the 1975 World Series, and cheered as the Reds beat the Yankees in four in 1976, the 1979 World Series is the one I remember best from my childhood. I couldn't believe that my team hadn't made it to the World Series in three years and that I would have to watch the Baltimore Orioles play the Pittsburgh Pirates. Of course I cheered for the Pirates, since they were more familiar to me. I was just beginning to learn the difference between the National and American Leagues, but I was sure that the National League was better. At that time I am not sure I even knew there was a team called the Orioles.

The American League was foreign, and being from southern Ohio, I rarely got to Indians games. Since Cleveland's stadium was always empty and Cincinnati's was always full, I was sure I had come to the right conclusion.

The Pittsburgh-Baltimore Series might have been the real beginning of my understanding of the game. Since I didn't really have any familiar "heroes" to root for on the field, I was able for the first time to really watch the game being played. Many young boys throughout the country attend games with their dads, who explain to them the intricacies of the sport. Aunt Mary and I never spoke about such matters, and I learned only by watching a lot.

The Reds fielded basically the same team for most of the 1970s, allowing me to become very familiar with them. I think often of kids growing up today, who become attached to players just as they are traded away. I think of the little boy who, when asked by Jason Giambi to name his favorite Yankee, replied "Tino Martinez," the player Giambi had been signed to replace. I do think we respond to a team when we become familiar with them as a team, maybe because they seem more like a family. To this day, I often revisit my old feelings about those players.

In 1998, when people compared the Yankees to the 1975 Reds, I felt a great sense of pride that they were referring to the same players that had drawn me to the sport. I had learned while watching the best. Watching the Yankees that year was like watching textbook baseball. Though I don't really remember many particular moments from the 1970s, I'm not sure any team will ever seem more amazing to me than the Reds of my youth.

From the very beginning, baseball teams have reflected the communities in which they played. Clubs originally sprang up to provide gentlemen with a place to enjoy each other's company while getting exercise and participating in the game, similar to today's country clubs with golf. Clubs would host neighboring sides for "baseball matches," which locals would attend. Having a good club brought pride to the entire community, and eventually clubs brought in more talented players to make themselves more competitive. These special players were awarded free membership to the club, and sometimes even financial rewards. Eventually all clubs paid their players in order to field the strongest and most talented teams possible and to bring accolades to their communities.

Spectators felt passionately about their hometown team and accepted players brought in from distant communities as true locals. At the time, people didn't relocate very often. Allegiance to a particular ball club was the norm, especially as professional teams were being formed. As teams became more expensive to field, it became important to build parks that could be roped off so the club could charge an admission fee. Thus, the business of baseball developed. It would be a few years before the game became recognized as a formal industry. All the participants in the business—players, coaches, owners, and general managers—would have significant impact on the shape that business took.

The uniforms the players wear have a definite significance. Early on, only thriving clubs could afford uniforms, and fan impressions of the team were largely based on how "professional" they looked. Harry Chadwick, an early baseball columnist for a New York paper, disdained the practice of changing uniforms as players moved around, since he felt it was the uniform that fans associated with a particular team. Uniforms demonstrated unity among a group of players.[1]

Though many Negro League and semi-pro teams experimented with uniform numbers throughout early baseball, The Indians were the first pro team to play a game with the digits on the backs of their uniforms. By the 1930s, all big-league clubs wore numbers. At first, the numbers corresponded to positions and were used for scoring. Later, Bill Veeck, as owner of the Chicago White Sox, added names to the backs of jerseys so fans could identify the players more easily, particularly on television. Other teams quickly followed suit. Charley Finley, in his stint as owner of the Athletics, introduced brightly hued gold and green uniforms to excite the eyes.

Recently, teams have discovered two benefits to changing uniform styles regularly. First, it allows the team to seem current as fashion trends change. Second, it creates marketing opportunities, as loyal fans buy new jerseys every few years to keep up to date. Fans often connect with the uniforms their team was wearing the first time they saw them in person. It is to the club's benefit to update fashion selectively, however, as changes to team colors can distance fans from the memories of their beloved team. For instance, the fans in San Diego on my visit in June 2002 wearing their old brown and gold jerseys looked disconnected from the red, white, and blue jerseys worn by the players on the field. The Padres again revamped their uniforms for 2004, to a sand and sky color scheme meant to reflect the Southern California surroundings, placing even more distance between themselves and the successful 1998 team that went all the way to the World Series.

The stadium is perhaps the most tangible and immediate factor in our perception of baseball in general, and our teams in particular. It is the park, after all, that introduces us to the professional game and indicates what we are to expect. Kids are especially sensitive to the differences between where they play the game and where the pros do. I remember watching two young boys enter Wrigley Field for their first major-league game in mid-August 2002. It was a beautiful Chicago day. Their eyes grew wide, and their mouths spread into broad smiles. The kids turned to their parents and began pulling their arms to hasten their journey through the stands to the edge of the field. Their excitement in seeing Wrigley was contagious. Though I had just seen nine games in nine days, I began to look around myself, feeling as if this were the first park I had ever laid eyes on.

For children of the 1950s and early 1960s raised on black-and-white television, visiting a stadium gave them their first chance to see the game in color. As they entered the confines of Ebbets Field, Yankee Stadium, or Wrigley, they saw how vibrant baseball could be. The grass was green, and the uniforms were blue. Some people in the upper deck of Shea still swear that the grass at Ebbets Field, the home of the Brooklyn Dodgers, was the greenest grass in the world. Andrew Blickstein, who grew up in New Jersey, attended Yankee games with his dad in the early 1970s. Yankee stadium is located in the Bronx, in what was then a dirty, burned-out neighborhood that must have seemed scary to a kid from the clean, beautiful suburbs. His most profound baseball memory from his childhood was entering the bleachers: "[They] would rise from the gate at the street level directly into the seating area. Your eyes would go from dirt and grime...through a small tunnel and arrive on a deep green field. I just couldn't believe that grass [that] pretty could grow in the Bronx."

The visual sensation of visiting a stadium in person was enhanced in the late 1960s and early 1970s, as all the new stadiums were made with brightly colored seats. The tradition of painting the seats goes back to the depression, when Larry McPhail purchased the Columbus Senators with the help of Branch Rickey, the general manager of the St. Louis Cardinals. The Senators were to become the AAA farm club for St. Louis. Though the team had been in decline for years, McPhail had many ideas for attracting fans. He renamed the team the Redbirds, and with professional players coming from the talented St. Louis club, he concentrated on marketing. Breaking with tradition, the first thing he did was paint the seats red and place redbirds on the outfield fence. McPhail would use similar tricks in other stadiums as he continued to try to turn around failing franchises throughout his baseball career.

The color of the seats may seem insignificant, yet it is a vivid part of the experience. During the Yankees/Mets series at Shea in 2002, a young kid behind me in line at the concession said to his father, "Isn't this a great place to see a game? The grass is so green, and all the colors..." His father, a Yankee fan, was not amused. But the colors at Shea are magic to young fans just as they were at the

Riverfront Stadium of my youth. When I attended the final games at Cinergy Field (the renamed Riverfront Stadium), I listened to people who had been coming for thirty years talk about the days when they sat in the "reds," the seats at the top level. As fans reminisced, many confessed that they had tried to sneak down from the "reds" to the "blues." It was a rite of passage in southern Ohio, and we knew exactly what these older fans meant.

The red seats in Busch Stadium provide a different effect, one that other teams would do well to be aware of. The Cardinals have a very loyal fan base, and if you visit the park you're likely to see many wearing red shirts sporting their favorite players' names. The effect is beautiful: the stands look like an ocean of red. From a distance, seats that are actually empty don't look empty at all; instead, they look as if they are filled with fans wearing red t-shirts. I'm sure that from the players' perspective, there are rarely many empty seats in Cardinal Land. Looking across the stadium, it didn't appear that there were any to me. St. Louis has approved the building of a new stadium, and the fans voted to keep the seats the traditional red instead of following the latest trend and installing hunter-green chairs.

The care a franchise takes with its stadium has a great deal to do with the fans' enjoyment of the game. In July 1965, a fan wrote *The Sporting News* to complain about the condition of Connie Mack Stadium:

"I wonder what it is like to enjoy a major-league game. [The] seats are narrow, dirty, and uncomfortable, the aisles are dirty, and the stands are peeling from lack of paint. [The] exits are cramped, [and the] ventilation is terrible in [the] restrooms."[2]

Like many fans in Montreal in 2002, this fan longed to see baseball played in a quality environment. A Seattle couple refused to go the Kingdome until they saw plans for Safeco field. Then they purchased season tickets to get preferential treatment when tickets for Safeco became available. Some franchises allow their stadiums to fall into disrepair so they can justify asking for a new one, but in some cases the fans they lose while this is happening may never return. In the case of Montreal, the quality of the stadium may have had more to do with the declining attendance then the passion locals felt for their team.

One thing that sets baseball apart from other sports is that each stadium is unique. The site and the team determine the fields' dimensions, even when the stands themselves are replicas of those in other stadiums. Football, basketball, and hockey all have specific dimensions for their playing area, whereas baseball specifies only the distance between the bases and between the pitcher and home plate. In the early days of baseball, fans could sit in stands or mill about in the outfield. There was no fence, so all of the home runs would technically be what we now call "inside the parkers." The players would go as far as they could to retrieve a ball, and during popular games that might have meant running into the crowd that had gathered behind them. Balls could get lost. There was a chance fans could obstruct the ball or cause injury to the player. This situation eventually changed, for a number of reasons. First, the owners discovered that if the field was open they couldn't charge people who chose to stand in the outfield throughout the game.[3] Second, outfielders often needed to contend with the fans for fly balls, and the owners recognized the physical threat posed by overzealous patrons.

The park is often referred to as the "tenth man" because of the effect the crowd has on the game. Today, with fans who are much more comfortable expressing their displeasure, the term is as relevant as ever. When we watch games in the Metrodome we can easily see how the domed roof lends to the unique experience, creating deafening noise levels that visiting teams may not be accustom to. Baseball teams are referred to as the home team and the visitors, echoing the sense of community we associate with the game. The tenth-man effect is one more element of the "home-field advantage," which when combined with a players familiarity with the peculiarities of the field, is far more relevant to the outcome of the game in baseball than any other sport. Football championships are often played in a neutral city, whereas baseball's World Series always takes place in the combatants' "home" stadiums.

Proximity to the action is another factor in the enjoyment of the game. The most successful stadiums provide intimacy and make fans feel as though they are a part of the action. I met a gentleman in Detroit who started going to Tigers games in 1944. "In Tiger Stadium," he said, "you were so close to the field." He admitted that the amenities in Comerica Park were better but insisted that "in all corners of the old place, you felt so close to the action." I suspect the average fan is afraid that this intimacy is the price we all must pay to create room for higher-priced luxury boxes. Proximity, though, is what makes "the friendly confines" of Wrigley Field so special. Along with closeness to the field, it is also important for fans to sit close to one another. Victor Brunetti, a Mets fan, mentioned that what makes him come back to Shea again and again is the potential to experience the stadium when "the seats are full and the crowd is into the game. It makes every pitch exciting and captures [his] attention and emotion." Size and configuration are clearly very important.

The ownership of the stadium also plays a part in the fans' experience. If fans contribute private funds towards the building of a stadium, they will feel a sense of ownership with it. If it is built with public money and the fans supported the levies, again, they can take pride in it. However, stadiums that are owned by corporations other than the team, or by out-of-town investors, create a sense of disenfranchisement among fans. For example, baseball fans at the Metrodome, which is owned by the Minnesota Vikings of the NFL, seemed more apprehensive about spending money there than fans did in places like Jacobs Field, where Indians reap the benefits of concession sales.

With the opening of so many new parks across the country, fans can take pride in the unique and special qualities that their home stadium possesses. This could be a classic quality, like that of an older stadium such as Wrigley, or it can be the stadium's comfort and amenities, such as those of Coors Field. Fans in Baltimore, home of the first successful "retro" park, express great pride in the feel of Camden Yards, which was for years considered the best park in the majors.

The rules that teams set within their stadiums also contribute to each park's unique feel. Seeing Barry Bonds put on a show during batting practice in Bank One Ballpark, crushing one ball after another down the right-field line, was highly memorable for me. Imagine a ten-year-old kid from Arizona seeing that for the first time, at his first professional game. It would be an experience unlike any other.

Now imagine that you are a Dodgers fan. Shawn Green has just matched the major-league (ML) record for home runs hit in a single game while on the road in Milwaukee. You convince your dad to take you to the next home game so that you can see your new hero. You arrive early, only to discover that the Dodgers do not admit fans to see the home team take batting practice (BP). The Dodgers are playing the Astros on this particular night, so you sit through Houston's batting practice. Brad Ausmus throws you a ball from the field and then signs it for you. You don't see Shawn Green until he takes center field an hour later, and he doesn't hit any home runs during the game. Now ask yourself: Which is the more meaningful memory, watching Shawn Green homer on television or having a big-league player take the time to sign your ball, wiggle your hat, and ask what position you play? Furthermore, Dodger Stadium makes you watch batting practice from the seat you purchased. If that seat is in the upper deck, that's where you sit during BP. How does a young fan ever get to see his or her favorite players up close and become familiar with them—maybe get an autograph—if they can't come down to the edge of the field, even for a short time? For many young fans, it's a great thrill to have a player stop for a moment to toss them a ball. Wouldn't a team rather that the player winning over a young fan be playing for the home organization? Wouldn't it be better for the team if the player who gave that young child such an experience played for them? Lou DePauli points out, "No matter how good TV coverage gets, there is still nothing like being there and getting a chance at a foul ball." Removing that chance, even during batting practice, removes the fans from the live experience.

The park can also add to the experience by enhancing the fan's knowledge of the game. At Turner Field, MLB's best family park, in my opinion, you will find Scout's Alley. Interspersed between food vendors are large pictures of past All-Star Games and blow-ups of famous Braves along with their scouting reports. In 2002, a fan could learn about Tom Glavine's performance when he was in high school before watching him pitch in the game. In Fenway, I sat next to a father with two teenage sons and a younger daughter. The sons loved sports, but the daughter wasn't interested at first—until we showed her the pitch clock, the retired numbers, and other features of the park that drew her in to the game. Many years ago, a fan wrote to *The Sporting News* to complain, "What's the use of going to a game when we go home wondering if Cramer was given a double or a single on his hit to center, and then have our kid brother tell us it was a single and an error. He heard the game on the radio. He knows. We don't. Why? Because we paid."[4] The fans in the stadium must be given more information than the fans at home watching on television. This will increase their knowledge of the game and make it more desirable to be in the stands. The sound system that a team uses, though, must be adequate for the stadium. Fans expect to be able to hear the announcements clearly, whether they have paid $12 or $120 for their ticket. The technology must be as current as possible, whether in an old stadium or a brand-new facility. Both Petco Park and Citizens Bank Stadium, two new parks in 2004, have state-of-the-art equipment, but the sound systems are inadequate when the stadiums are filled to capacity.

Mike Lupica won over some fans for baseball one day when he stopped across the street from Yankee Stadium, at Joseph J. Yancey Field, and volunteered to take thirty kids from the Morrisania Air Rights Community Center to the Yankees game that afternoon. As he recounts in his book, *Mad as Hell: How Sports Got Away from Fans and How We Can Get It Back*, he wasn't intending to be a hero; he simply decided that these kids probably wouldn't ever have the chance to see the inside of Yankee Stadium otherwise. He got thirty tickets and marched the kids, their chaperone, and her assistant into the stadium. One young man pointed at Paul O'Neill standing in the outfield, and another asked if that was where Babe Ruth had played. Lupica explained that Ruth had played there and that that was why the stadium was called the "House that Ruth Built."

"So Babe Ruth was in that same spot right there, where Paul O'Neill is?" the boy asked.

"The same spot," Lupica responded.

The kid smiled and said, "How great is that?"[5]

Even for these young fans, who had never seen a live game before, the connection to the past was strong.

Entering the confines of a stadium should allow the fans to breathe in the game, and it seems that most of the architects designing fields today agree. In many of the new stadiums, the concession area remains open to the field. Leaving the seating area to go to concessions can distance the fan from the game. Many of the older stadiums have tried to lessen this effect by hanging banners and large photos of former stars on the concourse. The older stadiums, Yankee, Fenway, and Wrigley, certainly can't change much, but the dank feeling that exists in the concession area does make the lines feel more oppressive and amplifies fan's removal from the field of play. Perhaps better lighting and some reminder of the setting would help. Seeing the palm trees in Miami or the New York skyline at Shea at least gives you a contextual background while standing in line that reminds you of where you are. Again, the murals at Turner Field, which are low enough for people to reach out and touch, are an effective use of space.

The ease with which people can reach their upper-deck seats is also an issue, especially now that ticket prices often preclude the average family from sitting anywhere else.

Ticket prices and packages are a huge factor in drawing fans. Though a team gains a large portion of its income from attendance and its ability to sell premium seats, it needs to understand that cultivating fans who buy tickets as adults is directly affected by the ability of kids to attend games during childhood. Recognizing this, some teams create half-price sections, while others offer packages that allow you to pay for a ticket and then receive free hot dogs and cokes. The Padres allow you to buy unsold tickets for certain games very cheaply, as long as you do so just a few weeks in advance. If MLB wants to continue attracting young people and families, going to a baseball game needs to be cheaper than going to a movie.

The stadiums that are spoken of most reverentially are the ones that place the focus on baseball. Wrigley is known for having no between-inning games, no lighted signage, and no Jumbotron. It is also the last stadium to play organ music only. Other parks still use an organ to create that antique quality, but they don't play organ music exclusively. Though most people I spoke to like a relatively quiet park, Patty Shaw mentioned that she enjoyed "the grounds crew doing the YMCA" routine at Yankee Stadium. Other fans enjoy hearing the songs that players pick to accompany their walk to the batter's box. For many, these songs give insight into the players themselves. For instance, you were reminded that

Rich Aurilia, the Giants shortstop in 2002, was a Brooklyn boy when he stepped up to the plate with the theme song from *The Sopranos* playing in the background.

The noise level between innings is intolerable to most. When asked what the team could do to make his experience better, Joe Balitewicz, a White Sox fan, replied, "Stop all the noise between batters!" Even Bernie Williams, center fielder for the Yankees, requested that no music be played during his at-bats in 2002 to allow him to concentrate. Carl Fortuna lamented, "The experience has diminished between innings. Somehow, loud music, such that you can barely hear yourself talk, is what must happen between innings. It is awful." Robert Lee Johnson wrote, "Many of us attend baseball games to relax, not to have our equilibrium further distorted by fanciful frenzies of hoopla and razzle-dazzle." It may be that parks are trying to masquerade the fact that breaks between innings have become progressively longer over the years to accommodate more television commercials when the game is broadcast. Even so, we need to find ways to keep people interested without bombarding them with noise unrelated to the action on the field. Perhaps a countdown clock in the stadium would be useful to let fans know how long they have until the action begins again, especially during playoff games, when the game is put on hold for the national audience. This would give fans an idea of how much time they had to visit the concessions or the restrooms between innings. Activities at the SkyDome, in Toronto, where cheerleaders pass out free shirts and certificates for hot dogs and other items, don't require a lot of loud music. The music is likely kept to a minimum because the dome has such an amplifying effect on any sound. Even with less than 20,000 fans in attendance, it is quite loud. Toronto does play commercials on the Jumbotron, though, and this is a problem for many fans. Rich Lamb, a Mets fan, bemoaned the feeling of being "battered by ads" at today's games. Simply put, high noise levels are anti-intuitive for a sport like baseball, which has always sought to be a comfortable, relaxing, and peaceful pastime.

In the past, teams have worked hard to create a special relationship with their fans, sometimes with appreciation nights in which teams join with local sponsors to offer meaningful gifts, especially for less popular games. However, teams need to find other ways to make fans feel special. In 1971, the Cincinnati Reds chose two fans from the stands at random to help the team hoist the 1970 National League Championship flag above Riverfront. These weren't special guests or friends of the team, but rather regular Joes who had purchased tickets and had simply come down to root for the Reds.

Master promoter Bill Veeck once received a letter written by Joe Early wondering why the regular fan doesn't get honored before a game. Veeck decided it was a great idea and gave that fan his own night, Joe Early Night, before a St. Louis Browns game. In 1966, the Baltimore Orioles ran a fan-relations department in 1966. There they fielded suggestions and complaints, making fans feel as though their voices were being heard. Teams are reluctant to do this often because many of the complaints they receive relate to issues they are already aware of but cannot rectify; however, it is nice for fans to know that the team is aware of problems and is trying to address them. As the fan is feeling more lost in the business of baseball, this feedback from the team can be an educational tool about issues derived from union or league rules, as well.

Many fans describe the appeal of watching a game where their father watched a game. Much of the mystique of places like Fenway and Wrigley is that generations have gone there to do exactly what we go there to do. The interest our parents and grandparents had in the game is often passed on to us there. Howie Abrams told me of his "favorite person in the world growing up," his grandfather, taking him to Mets games. When I stood in the stands on the North Side of Chicago, I envisioned myself surrounded by men in fedoras and ladies in pearls, there for an afternoon game in the 1940s. Wrigley definitely exudes the feel of times gone by.

An entire generation of fans in New York chose the Mets as their team because their fathers had hated the Yankees—and because the Dodgers and Giants had left to go west. The Mets moved to town to fill the void and adopted the colors of the teams that they were trying to replace, taking the blue of the Dodgers and the orange of the Giants. Brendan White is an example of one of these Mets fans. His father loved all sports, and his grandfather really loved to talk about baseball. The family had been Brooklyn Dodgers fans, and his grandfather even had worked at Ebbets Field in the 1920s. They hated the Yankees, so Brendan naturally became a Mets fan. He remembers going to games and seeing Willie Mays play at the end of his career. The traditions—and the memories of the traditions—that begin with our families often stay with us forever. Louis DePauli, from St. Clair, Pennsylvania, told me that his Uncle Mike had worked for the railroad and would take him on trips to see the Phillies play in Connie Mack Stadium. They had a tradition: they would watch BP and then move to their seats and sit there the entire time, no matter what. Even if their seats were behind a pole and there was no one else in the stadium, they would remain in the seats that they had purchased.

The stadium itself is the most controllable aspect of the fan experience. All experiences of the game are mediated by the comfort of the fan and how easy it is for them to be there. With ticket prices becoming increasingly exorbitant, fans need to feel they are getting more than the opportunity to see, as one British observer pointed out, "a whole lot of almost fat blokes running around and getting paid millions of dollars to do so." They want to feel comfortable and not hassled. The park should serve as an escape from the stresses of everyday life, a calm place to relax on a day off from work. With other forms of entertainment vying for our dollars, baseball needs to examine the unique niche it can fill. By harkening back to the days of our parents, or to our own childhood, while using modern technology to enhance the experience, the game can become special to a whole new generation. People, longing for the simple life, will always seek it out.

2

Circling the Bases: Part 1

I began my journey around the majors in April and completed visits to the first six stadiums by the end of May, mostly taking long-weekend trips as I vacationed from my full-time job. I had planned out the entire summer, grouping teams together by geography and planning around their schedules. I scheduled the biggest groups, such as the California teams, first, followed by a group consisting of Chicago, Milwaukee, and Minnesota. The rest just fell into place.

I began in Florida and Atlanta for purely selfish reasons, thinking it would be pleasant to watch games in warm weather in April. What I didn't know was that the two Florida teams would be excellent benchmarks for understanding the function of the stadiums and the importance of the fans. I had the opportunity to see their well-publicized problems first hand, and later on I would see how established clubs dealt with the same issues. I also came to understand quickly that I couldn't expect to compare the Florida Marlins to the New York Yankees. History separates them. It is, however, important to note the differences between the Florida Marlins and other expansion teams, particularly how well those teams did in their sixth year of existence. With baseball, the trick of it is to look at its present-day circumstances in the context of what has happened in the history of the game. We are comfortable with this when talking about hitting streaks and home run records, but I think this model also needs to be applied to the successes and failures of the franchises themselves.

The reasons fans have for loving the game vary widely, depending on the history of the local team and the access the individual has to other teams. As I dissected each franchise, I tried on one level to understand the frustrations and joys of fans in each stadium, but I also looked at the issues that affected all the clubs. I also tried to keep in mind that circumstances change throughout the course of a regular season. A team might have been strong contenders in April, but by the time I visited in July, they may have traded away their entire starting pitching staff, disappointing the local fans. It's all about context.

Tropicana Field
Toronto Blue Jays @ Tampa Bay Devil Rays
April 12, 2002
Box 110, Row R, Seat 1A

Tropicana Field, in Tampa Bay, was built either to lure an existing Major League Baseball team wishing to relocate or to win franchise rights prior to the 1991 expansion. There had been earlier attempts to purchase the White Sox and the Mariners, but nothing came of it. Finally, two Tampa investors attempted to purchase the San Francisco Giants from owner Bob Lurie who was having personal financial troubles at the time. Major League Baseball vetoed the sale, citing concerns about the backgrounds of the investors and a desire to keep the Giants in San Francisco. Lawsuits followed, and upon their completion, the Florida attorney general filed suit against MLB on the grounds that it had violated anti-trust laws by preventing the move of the Giants to Florida. It seems that MLB chose Tampa Bay as an expansion team to squelch further lawsuits and to appease Florida lawmakers, fearing that its anti-trust exemption might be challenged.[6] Tampa Bay was granted a franchise in March of 1995. The club would play its inaugural season in 1998, the same year that the Arizona Diamondbacks would begin play. That year they sold out opening day in seventeen minutes and by mid-April they had a winning record, becoming the first team ever to be four games above .500 at any time in their first season of play.

Tropicana Field was the only turf stadium to have dirt base paths. In the off-season between 1999 and 2000, actual Field Turf was installed to simulate all the characteristics of a real grass field. It is the only indoor baseball stadium to use Field Turf, which is a vast improvement over the green carpeting used in other indoor stadiums. This simulated grass allows the ball to bounce and roll as it would on a grass outfield.

When I arrived at Tropicana Field, I didn't know what to expect. Tampa Bay had started the same year as the Diamondbacks, the expansion team that had won the World Series in 2001, but the Devil Rays had lost one hundred games the previous season and attendance was reportedly meager. I knew little about the Tampa Bay squad. I knew Greg Vaughn had landed there after his stint with the Reds, though he would be released early in the 2002 season. As for the visitors, the Toronto Blue Jays, I knew that they had a couple of strong players that might become stars if given the chance to play for a different team. The American

League East, to which both of these teams belonged, was a tough division. The Yankees and the Red Sox dominated on the field and in the headlines.

When I entered Tropicana Field, I was surprised to discover an air of excitement inside. I immediately found some friendly ushers in the outfield seats, shagging balls to give to young fans. One of these men, Sam, immediately greeted me and handed me a ball. He had lived in Pittsburgh and had followed the Pirates up until he retired in Florida. He called for Ben Greive to toss me a ball, and the right fielder pleasantly complied. There were not many people at the game this early, nor would many more arrive before the first pitch. The upper deck had been closed off to keep staffing to a minimum.

It quickly became evident that the team had many ardent, loving fans. One man I met had arranged his delivery route with his boss so he could finish near the stadium each day in time to catch the evening's game. How many teams with strings of losing seasons have inspired such loyalty? Many of the people sitting around me were originally from some other city—mostly New York, it seemed. Though they recognized that their team was young, they were frustrated by the team's inability to execute. Their thorough understanding of the game was apparent as they critiqued the players' base running and pick-off moves.

The game didn't really have the air of Major League Baseball, due to both the skill level on the field and the atmosphere in the stands. It was a high-scoring see-saw game: the Devil Rays would score a couple of runs, then the Blue Jays would score twice as many, then the Rays would score a few more. By the bottom of the sixth, the score was 8-6 in favor of the Jays. In the seventh, the Jays took off, scoring four more runs, and at that point the Devil Rays seemed stunned. The energy in the stands dissipated. For six innings, the team had played pretty good ball, but it was clearly over when the Jays made the score 12-6. In the eighth, Toronto scored twice more, to end it 14-6.

There was scoreboard watching all around me. Most people were following the Yankees' progress in Boston, and the reactions were mixed. Some were rooting for New York and some against them. This early-season attention to the out-of-town games surprised me, yet it made some sense. Though most people in the stands were rooting for Tampa Bay, the lack of skill on the field made it difficult to cut the ties to their former teams, especially the Yankees, who had recently had great success. The people at this game had a real appreciation for the game and stayed for the entire nine innings. They will continue to come even if the Devil Rays lose another one hundred games, because they want to see the game played locally. They won't be fans of the local team, however, until the local team gives them something to cheer about.

At Tropicana, the activities between innings were kept to a minimum, though many encouraged fan involvement. One less successful contest involved a fan, a golf pro, and right-handed pitcher Tanyon Sturtze, who left the team following the 2002 season. It involved a golf game in the outfield, with the object being to hit the ball as close to a flag as possible. In the end, Tanyon Sturtze was closest and received a gift certificate for a weekend of golfing. The fan and the pro received an autograph from Sturtze. The patrons around me all agreed that the autograph was silly, since the real prize was going to someone well compensated for the game. If the purpose of promotions is to inspire people to come to the field, shouldn't the games be set up so that the fan either can't lose or at least is the one to leave with the best prize? Sturtze represented the club in the contest, at least from the fan's perspective. A better idea would have been not to give away the free round and let another fan try for it the next night. This would allow for greater fan involvement and further promotional opportunities for the company donating the gift. Sturtze might not have been available every night, but having different players with different skill levels could have added to the fun, allowing fans a glimpse into what the players were like off the field.

What many don't realize is that players are not required in their contracts to make appearances on behalf of the club. If Sturtze were asked to partake in the contest without the chance of winning the free round of golf, would he have accepted? We'll talk further about this problem down the line, but the point is that clubs need to make the fans feel important. Joe Balitewicz suggested that clubs should "let real people throw out the first pitch." In doing so, they would bring the fan to the front and center to the game experience.

I found Tropicana Field friendly and comfortable, with lots of selection regarding food and ticket prices and an excellent sound system for a dome. For those in the stands, it seemed geared towards creating a pleasant experience. Though the dome is practical in that it protects the games from Florida's unpredictable weather, it has the inherent problem of keeping fans from the natural feel of baseball played under the open sky. Though the dome does serve to make the spectators comfortable, it also takes away an element that might be essential for those of us that grew up in the game; to remind us of that feeling we had as a child when entering the stands.

I was in Tampa in April of 2002, while the Masters golf tournament was taking place in Augusta, Georgia. Prior to each Friday-night home game that season, Chuck LaMar, senior vice president of baseball operations and general manager of the Devil Rays, participated in a one-hour call-in show on the local sports talk radio station. During this particular program, Mr. Lamar was continually interrupted by updates from Augusta. He was patient, and the disruption didn't seem to bother him. This clearly demonstrated both his willingness to connect with fans and his understanding of his fan base. I tried to imagine a general manager of another team being so gracious, but I couldn't think of another city where the talk show would have considered another sport to take precedence over a general manager's time.

While apathy is a large part of the attendance problem for the Devil Rays, clearly the love of golf in Florida is also a factor. The dome hurts the Devil Rays' ability to attract fans in an area like Florida, where many people move so they can take advantage of the outdoor activities. When the weather is beautiful, people don't want to watch an outdoor sport in an artificial setting. Because of this, golf will continue to eat into baseball's fan base here, and the Rays will continue to have a difficult time nurturing it. The off-season moves in the winter following the 2002 season—including the acquisition of one of the most successful managers in the game today, Lou Piniella—will generate some excitement and definitely lead to larger crowds. While Piniella's ability to steer a young team in the right direction, to inspire respect, and to demonstrate his strong feelings of loyalty to his players might help the Devil Rays fill seats, Tampa Bay management must continue to work at creating excitement in the stadium. Free golf weekends might be an incentive, but success on the field is the key.

Pro Player Stadium
Atlanta Braves @ Florida Marlins
April 13, 2002
Section 144, Row 13, Seat 11

In 1985, baseball completed its collective bargaining agreement (CBA) with the Major League Baseball Players Association (MLBPA), which among other things allowed the National League to expand by two teams. MLB announced that it would charge $190 million for a franchise. At the end of 1990, MLB revealed that its shortlist of locations being considered consisted of Buffalo, Denver, Orlando, South Florida, Tampa-St. Petersburg, and Washington, D.C.

The Florida Marlins, originally owned by H. Wayne Huizenga, were granted a franchise in July 1991 for the 1993 season. Huizenga, as CEO of Blockbuster Video, had been hired to produce the video releases for MLB prior to his selection as an owner. With Tampa Bay already having built a stadium, many were surprised when Huizenga's proposal to bring baseball to Miami was accepted.

However, the Miami area had had a great history of semi-pro baseball, including the Marlins of the 1950s, with legendary hurler, Satchel Paige as part of the team.

With its large Cuban population, among which baseball is hugely popular, Miami seemed a perfect fit for a MLB franchise. Huizenga's previous business relationship with MLB certainly made the prospect of his ownership more appetizing to the other owners. In their first season, the modern Florida Marlins drew over 3 million fans. That total has not been reached since, however, neither during their World Series Championship year of 1997, when they became the first wildcard team to compete in the October Classic, nor during their 2003 World Series year. Those two years, in fact, are the only ones in their history in which they have won more games than they have lost.

Perhaps because attendance did not meet expectations, despite the team's success on the field, the 1997 team was broken up and its stars were traded for lower salaried players. Locals quickly became disenchanted, and the team was sold to businessman John Henry two years after their World Series victory. This second owner's group wanted a new stadium built for them, but refused to make any real threat to relocate if this did not happen. Local supporters no longer felt they needed to do anything to assist him and continually voted against stadium levies. John Henry, frustrated by this and lacking the private backing to build a stadium for an unpopular team, began looking for a buyer. The team was sold in 2002 to the former owner of the Montreal Expos, Jeffery Loria. Bearing the fruit of their farm system they were once again able to win the National League pennant as the wild card, and they went on to beat the Yankees in the 2003 World Series.

The Marlins play in what is now named Pro Player Stadium. Originally named Joe Robbie Stadium (also the home of the Miami Dolphins), it was purchased by Huizenga to help secure the rights to a franchise. Though seats have been removed to create a deeper left field, the outfield field-level seats are angled for football and do not give the fan a comfortable view of the batter. The stadium is full of color and tantalizes the senses, but it lacks any sense of intimacy, and the players seem very far away. The new ownership attempted to address this in 2003 by closing the upper deck for all but a few games. By precluding the purchase of upper-deck tickets, the Marlins are shepherding their fans together. This can only help create a sense of community as fans cheer for their team.

The biggest problem with Pro Player is the Florida sun, which during baseball season makes the wind-sheltered stadium feel like an oven. The expensive seats in Florida are under the overhang, in the shade, and I imagine in July they are well worth their price. Unfortunately, this puts the premium-seat buyer far away from the action, potentially alienating fans willing to pay the higher-end ticket prices.

Because this stadium serves a dual purpose, it is difficult to create the atmosphere of baseball throughout. It feels as if the Marlins are unwanted visitors, with the concourse devoid of any baseball imagery. With the exception of the palm trees outside the stadium, you may even forget you are in Florida. There is an area of the stands in center field, referred to as "the fish tank," whose tickets are less than half the price of those for other sections. It's one reminder of the locale of the team, but why not create more? How about an area in the outfield where beach umbrellas block the sun? If no atmosphere exists, a team needs to create one to make the fans' experience special and comfortable.

The stadium has carried a number of policies over from football to baseball that affect the game experience. The Marlins, along with a couple of other stadiums, have instituted what they call a "courtesy rule." This rule states that if you leave your seat to visit the concessions or the bathroom, you won't be allowed back into the seating area until the batter has finished his turn at bat and the play is complete. This is meant to prevent people from moving around the stands during an at-bat and disturbing others. In football, this works only because each play is so brief, with a lot of time between plays. In baseball, however, it doesn't work at all. On one occasion I was allowed to return to my seat after a play, yet I didn't arrive at the end of my row until after the next batter had stepped into the batter's box, meaning I still disturbed my row during an at-bat. The rule ensures that the returning spectator disturbs his or her row no matter what, despite the fact that the person visiting the concession misses an at-bat while waiting to return to the seating area. Football and baseball are very different sports; automatically carrying over policies from one to the other doesn't seem like a good idea.

Attendance during the two games in Florida varied greatly between the Saturday night game and the Sunday afternoon game. The first game was pretty well populated with fans of the visiting team, the Atlanta Braves. Florida had been Braves country for a very long time prior to the arrival of Marlins baseball in Florida, and the number of Braves jerseys proved that things had not changed drastically. I was hard pressed to find a Marlins shirt in the stands, despite the announced attendance of over 18,000. With so many Braves fans present, it was easy to forget who the home team was. The game was neck and neck throughout, eventually going fourteen innings, and the Braves fans were so numerous that they were able to start up a version of the "tomahawk chop", a chant-and-arm movement meant to create the feeling of warring Braves surrounding the enemy. In Atlanta, this cheer can be intimidating to the visiting team, but when done by the visiting fans in another team's park, the effect is completely demoralizing. As someone rooting for the Marlins, I was certainly intimidated, though I recognized that the Atlanta fans were merely embracing a Braves tradition that they would rarely be able to participate in from their homes in Florida. Creating a unique fan cheer might be the next step towards drawing Florida fans into the experience. Also, giving fans a reason to attend games against the Braves wearing Marlins garb might create a common bond and give Florida home-field advantage again.

The next day I searched more intently for Marlins fans, and though there were fewer people at the game, a larger proportion were rooting for Florida. Prior to the game, I met a man with his family from North Carolina who had become a Marlins fan. He had grown up an Orioles fan and had continued to follow them until his son was born, in 1993, the Marlins' inaugural year. The father decided at that time to start a new tradition of rooting for the Marlins, something his family could grow into together. Until this point, I had a bias against expansion teams, but now I suddenly saw the advantage of expansion. It is more than just a means to reap money from potential baseball fans too far removed from a present major-league market; it also gives fans the opportunity to come together and share a history, to connect with other fans.

This story created a warm feeling in me towards the Marlins, and so I went off to search for a souvenir. Unfortunately, this proved difficult. I walked around the entire stadium and found only one open concession where one could purchase a Marlins t-shirt. The store was tiny, and the selection was minimal. I now understood why there were so few Marlins shirts in the stands. Over the next couple of days, I searched outside the stadium for Marlins merchandise, including the Wal-Mart and the airport. I eventually came to realize that there was no buzz about the Marlins because promotional materials were so scarce. Team apparel creates a sense of belonging to a group that can only raise interest in the team.

Now, as I am writing about my experience, I only vaguely remember why it is that for that afternoon I really did care about the fortunes of the Marlins. The answer is that both Marlins/Braves games were great. The first was very close, with the Braves pulling ahead 4-1 in the top of the fourth and the Marlins making it 4-3 in the bottom of that inning, and then tying it up with a couple of singles, a wild pitch and an error in the sixth. The game remained tied for a very long time.

According to current rules, all Major League Baseball teams are required to stop selling beer after the seventh inning. During this game, the team closed all concessions. In the tenth inning, fans were frustrated to discover that they couldn't buy another Coke, popcorn, or hotdog. In the twelfth, I had to go to the bathroom and fill up an old cup just to get some water. Certainly management should realize that although some of the vendors should close down following the seventh, especially when attendance is poor, fans need and want to be comfortable for the entire game. If it's more comfortable to watch the game on the television in their living room, that's what the average fan is going to do. The message to the fans that night was that they should go home—that's certainly what the Marlins staff was doing. It's a joy of baseball that there is no clock, yet that idea needs to apply to all aspects of the live experience.

Prior to this game, Andrew Feirstein, coordinator of media relations for the Marlins, told me that what happens "between the lines" is what draws in fans. During my two days in Florida, I saw some great baseball. The Marlins won the first game 5-4 in fourteen innings. The second game, A. J. Burnett pitched a four-hit complete-game shutout that the Marlins won 7-0. In the paper the next day, there was much less discussion about the Marlins than there was about the University of Florida Hurricanes baseball team, which had failed to make the college playoffs for the second time in two years after a tremendous ten-year run.

At the end of the season, the Marlins had played nearly .500 baseball with a very young team. Luis Castillo had gone on a thirty-five-game hitting streak, the longest in the majors since Paul Molitor's in 1987 and the tenth longest in history. The entire starting pitching staff, though young, pitched very well when they were healthy. Yet on the last day of the season, the Marlins were in danger of having the worst season attendance in the league. Clearly, it is not just what happens "between the lines" that matters. It's the total fan experience that determines whether someone is going to spend his or her money at the stadium. And it is management's willingness or unwillingness to spend money that determines what kind of team the fans will be watching.

In 2003, the Marlins were able to bring a young pitcher up from the minors when A. J. Burnett required season-ending surgery. This pitcher, Dontrelle Willis, with his unique delivery, was able to surprise and confuse opposing batters and had great success for the first part of the season. Fans started buying tickets to see this phenom do his stuff. After hiring a new manager in May and committing the fewest errors in the National League, the team began to play better and better. The Marlins also made a commitment to the team at the trading deadline, as teams in the hunt went looking for a talented third baseman. The Marlins had one, Mike Lowell, who was nearing free agency. The team made a public commitment not to trade him and to build the team around him. This was the first sign that ownership was interested in building a contender and not just maintaining a low-budget team. The Marlins ended up being part of one of the most exciting races of the year and won the wild card in the last week of the season.

The team was able to sell out the stadium for all of its post-season games—not just the lower level, but the entire stadium. Now, with success to build on, the new Marlin ownership really has the opportunity to nurture its fan base. Only time will tell if they are capable of capitalizing on this opportunity.

Turner Field
Florida Marlins @ Atlanta Braves
April 19, 2002
Section 108, Row 10, Seat 9

The third stop on my odyssey was Turner Field, home of the Atlanta Braves. Originally known as the Red Stockings in Boston, the team joined the National League in 1876. In those days, team monikers were often merely nicknames given by sportswriters that the local papers picked up, and they often changed. In 1883, the Red Stockings became known as the Beaneaters. In 1907, their name changed to the Doves, after their new owners, the Dovey brothers. Finally, in 1912, they became known as the Braves. The Red Sox, the American League team in Boston, became very popular following their World Series victory in 1918, and then again during their appearance in the Series of 1946. All of baseball enjoyed rejuvenated attendance after the war, but by the early 1950s the second team in many Eastern cities was struggling, including the Boston Braves. Following the war, the population began to shift westward, and only the largest Eastern cities were able to support more than one franchise.

Lou Perini, owner of the Braves, also owned Milwaukee's minor-league rights. After squelching an opportunity for the St. Louis Browns to move to Milwaukee and into a brand-new publicly funded stadium, Perini decided to move the Braves there from Boston in 1953. It turned out to be a great move for the franchise. In just thirteen games, more fans in Milwaukee had headed through the turnstiles than in the entire previous season in Boston. In their second season in the new city, the Braves featured a young rookie who would achieve great fame by setting the major-league homerun record. His name was Hank Aaron. The team would win pennants in 1957 and 1958 and would set National League records for attendance. But by the early 1960s, attendance began to drop off, as did the success of the team. The Braves would remain in Milwaukee until 1966, when Atlanta, by also publicly funding a new stadium and offering the hope of capturing the hearts and dollars of the entire South, would lure the team away from Milwaukee.

In their inaugural season as the Atlanta Braves, the team drew 1.5 million fans, but it also earned $2.5 million dollars in television revenues, significantly more than they had garnered in Milwaukee. Despite his team's lack of success, Hank Aaron continued his drive to become the homerun king, finally matching Babe Ruth on April 4, 1974, and passing him seventeen days later. In 1976, Ted Turner purchased the club. That same year, the Turner Broadcasting Station (TBS) became the first nationwide cable "Superstation" and began airing all Atlanta Braves games on cable television. After many dismal years in Atlanta, the Braves would become "the team of the nineties" by appearing in the post season thirteen times and the World Series five times between 1991 and 2004. They would win it only once, in 1995. In 2001, Turner Broadcasting merged with AOL/Time Warner, and the Braves got new owners.

In 1996, Atlanta played host to the Olympic Games. A stadium was built, for the track-and-field events, which would eventually become the new home of the Braves.

Turner Field was the first park I entered in the 2002 season that gave me the impression that baseball was *meant* to be played there. The experience begins outside the park, with a courtyard area around the ticket office full of statues of the great Braves in history: Eddie Matthews, Warren Spahn, Phil Neikro, and, of course, Hank Aaron. It also features an impressive statue of Ty Cobb, known as the Georgia Peach. Besides honoring a great baseball player, the statue celebrates the tradition of baseball in Georgia and creates a historical connection between the Braves and its adopted city.

The gates open three hours before game time in Atlanta, allowing access to food concessions, the team store (the largest in the majors, I think), and the outfield seats. For me, the entrance felt a lot like that of an amusement park, and I was particularly disappointed by AOL/Time Warner's need to cross-promote, especially with the Cartoon Network. Characters roamed the plaza greeting young fans. The team store, in the center of the plaza, contains all the Braves merchandise you could possibly desire. Outside the team store are picnic tables and a number of televisions tuned to other baseball games around the country, allowing one to buy food and enjoy a picnic before the game while keeping track of the other teams around the league. For me, this built a sense of anticipation. It was exciting to watch the other teams on television while knowing that I would soon be watching the Braves play live.

The Braves have also found a compromise between giving the home team privacy while they take batting practice and giving the fans access to the players. They only allow fans into the outfield bleachers until the Braves are done. Kids can still catch fly balls and call out to their favorite players, yet those players can steer away from those sections as well. There is something inspiring about standing in the outfield seats and looking back at the empty stadium, especially as ushers begin to step into place. One can imagine how we as fans appear to players standing on the field. A single usher in the upper tier looks pretty small against the backdrop of those mammoth stands.

There is one other thing that the Braves do well that might benefit a team like the Marlins. The Braves offer a lot of ticket choices and packages. There are seats for $5 on the day of the game in the beer garden in the outfield, and there are $2 seats in the extreme upper deck rows. The variety of ticket packages makes baseball accessible to anyone and encourages the last-minute ticket buyer. Of course, the seats behind home plate are considerably more expensive. With this pricing schedule, a baseball game in Atlanta is almost as economical a form of entertainment as renting a movie at home.

When the rest of the stands finally opened as the Marlins took batting practice,—yes, I watched the Braves play in Miami and then the Marlins play in Atlanta—I discovered Scout's Alley, the concourse around the infield seats. When you leave the seating area at older parks, you become detached from the atmosphere of the game, no matter how many televisions are placed around the concessions. At Turner Field, this isn't true. The concourse is a little dark, especially compared to the bright Georgia sunshine in the field, but the amusement-park atmosphere that you find near the entrance is focused here on the game of baseball.

I knew these games would be great after seeing the same two teams compete the weekend before. At the first game on Friday night, the stands were filled with Braves hats and shirts. I sat behind three businessmen; two had grown up as Braves fans and the third was a Cubs fan from Chicago. One of the gentlemen had been at Fulton County Stadium, the previous home of the Braves in Atlanta, on the day when Hank Aaron tied Babe Ruth's homerun record. These fellows teased me about being from New York, since the Braves and the Mets had a bit of a rivalry. I promised to try to root for the home team as long as no one around me felt the need to do the tomahawk chop, and they laughed.

In Atlanta, there are a lot of demonstrations of team pride. Everyone owns a shirt or a cap and all the locals seem to have been fans for a very long time. The number of fans under twenty-five is impressive, yet it is not surprising considering the team's success throughout the 1990s and the city's population growth over the past twenty years. Their record during that time, and the loyalty of their fan base, can only be compared to that of the Yankees or Cardinals.

One hears a lot about the fickleness of Braves fans, however. For the last three years, the team has failed to sell out playoff games. The fans I spoke with seemed to expect the Braves to win and felt connected to the team even if they didn't attend the games. My guess is that the team plays such a high caliber of baseball throughout the year that they don't seem to play any better when the stakes are higher. Whereas the level of play elsewhere rises dramatically during the playoffs, in Atlanta it seems like just another day at the ballpark.

I also detected a general lack of baseball knowledge among many Atlanta fans. During a tie game, in the bottom of the eighth with Keith Lockhart on third, Rafael Furcal on second, and Andruw Jones at the plate, the fans had grown bored. They had started the wave at the top of the inning, and it now was going very well. Fans were participating in the best wave I've ever seen; yet Andruw Jones was battling the count, trying to get a base hit and the game-winning RBI. It was one of the best at-bats I had ever witnessed, with Jones fouling off pitch after pitch, yet the fans simply weren't watching. They didn't seem to appreciate the epic battle between pitcher and batter. As the wave of fans rose to their feet, I couldn't help wondering if this distracted both the batter and the pitcher. Granted, part of the appeal of home-field advantage is the ability to distract the other team, but it must also have been difficult for Andruw Jones to concentrate on the pitcher's release point with so much movement happening all around him. In the end, he hit into a fielder's choice, the out was made at the plate, and the Braves lost a chance to move ahead on the scoreboard.

A late-inning tie ball game is about as tense as it gets in baseball. The excitement of having your best player up at the plate with the winning run on base would cause most fans to lean forward in their seats. In Atlanta, however, there was little excitement. Only winning itself seems to matter. Sitting in the stands, I felt the fans' love for the idea of a winning team but not for the game itself. The Braves need to raise the drama of late-inning situations, using the scoreboard and video screen to place the focus back onto the field. The atmosphere in the stadium is the most baseball oriented in the majors; the next step is to take the enthusiasm demonstrated by that wave and focus it on the team. This may help to remedy the lack of interest in the post-season as well.

Coors Field
Atlanta Braves @ Colorado Rockies
April 17, 2002
Section 123, Row 12, Seat 8

In January of 1991, following the announcement that Denver had made the short list of possible cities to gain a MLB franchise, the city of Denver kicked off a season ticket drive, asking people to commit $50 as a deposit, refundable if Denver's bid was unsuccessful. This was a huge success and one of the biggest factors in MLB's decision to select Colorado as its next expansion franchise six months later. The Colorado Rockies already had such a fan following when pro baseball started playing in Denver that their franchise holds most MLB attendance records. This is partially because they began playing in Mile High Stadium, a football venue with more seats than a traditional baseball stadium, but even after the smaller Coors Field was built the team continued to draw more fans than most other franchises, despite posting few winning seasons.

The Rockies began play in 1993, the same year as the Florida Marlins. Colorado was the first team to lead the majors in attendance while finishing last in the standings. Denver had never had a Major League Baseball team, though they had enjoyed barnstorming teams in the 1940s and 1950s. Bill, an usher at Coors Field, remembered the Kansas City Monarchs coming through to play a local team. Satchel Paige had pitched for the Monarchs. "He was great, but the hitters on his team were so good that they would bat through the side almost every inning," he said.

I was excited to see Coors Field, having heard so many wonderful descriptions of it. A pair of Chicago men that I had met in Miami who were traveling to ballparks around the majors had described its view of the mountains as "spectacular." They suggested I sit on the first-base side to watch the sun set behind the mountains. Two other guys, who had visited every venue in MLB, the NBA, the NFL, and the NHL in 2002, complained that the setting sun had blinded them and hindered their view of the game. Again I was learning it was all about perspective.

I arrived at my hotel a few hours before game time to discover a throng of people gathered outside the hotel. I checked in, settled into my room, and returned to the curb to find out what had drawn them there. The Braves, who were the visiting team this evening, were staying here, and the people gathered outside were autograph seekers. Though several of them were collectors and autograph hounds trying to make a profit, most were actually fans of the Braves. Due to the broadcast of all of Atlanta's games on TBS throughout the country, it seems that everyplace that doesn't host a team has become Braves' territory and baseball fans in the far reaches of the mountain states had come to Denver to see their team play up close. Outside the stadium, I saw a sea of red and blue caps and shirts. People I spoke with had driven from Las Vegas ("You know, Maddux is from Las Vegas"), Nebraska, and even Montana. These fans had planned their vacations around this series.

I worried at first that these games would be like the Marlins games, with Braves fans outnumbering the locals, but by game time I realized my fears had been unnecessary. The stands were nearly full of transplants who had shifted their allegiances and embraced the Rockies. At times, the Braves fans were a bit louder than the Rockies fans, and it seemed as if the home team fans were waiting for cues on the scoreboard to cheer. Though many fans had come from other MLB cities, these fans were merging their former cheering styles. The scoreboard did a lot of prompting, and the fans happily followed its lead. At times, fans from the East would heckle with familiar cracks from Shea or Comiskey, but in general, the fans were coming together as a group and finding middle ground in their various styles of cheering. It quickly became apparent that the Rockies were succeeding in creating a common language needed for bonding that the Florida Marlins were missing.

Coors Field is one of the more beautiful stadiums in baseball, as I had heard. It feels very much like Turner Field, except that the concourse is open to the field. You are never far away from the action, unless you are sitting in the section known as the "rock pile." It was a bit hazy the weekend I was there, so I missed out on the spectacular views, but the stadium was so comfortable that I didn't mind.

Coors Field was built in what had been an abandoned part of town on unused railroad tracks. The area has come alive since, though, with pubs and clubs opening up along the street. The team has helped revitalize an area that had died off, creating some exciting downtown nightlife. Since there is so much to do around the stadium, fans no longer need the team to win to consider the night out a success. Going to a Rockies game might be a small part of a fan's plan for the night, which benefits both the team and the city, ensuring the team's place in the community. Coors Field might be the best example of how a sports franchise can revitalize a downtown area. It has helped the community flourish and is perhaps one of the few instances where public funding has been justified.

Beginning in the 2002 season, however, the club began to have trouble filling the seats. They had spent some big money on a few players, and the lack of success on the field, as well as tremendous success of the other local professional sports franchises, was causing attendance to drop. On April 26, 2002, Buddy Bell was fired as the manager of the Rockies. Dan O'Dowd, the Rockies' general manager, was quoted as saying that he needed to do something "to capture the imagination of the fans."[7] The Rockies' record did improve slightly, though many of the high-priced players continued to perform poorly.

There was no dramatic turnaround in attendance figures, and it soon became apparent that Bell's firing had no effect on the fans' willingness to purchase tickets. Mike Hampton, a pitcher earning $15 million a year, couldn't win a game, and he could not be traded or released due to his exorbitant salary. Bell could be released, however, and though he hadn't been responsible for Hampton's inability to win, he was asked to move along in the hope that any change might demonstrate that the front office was trying to keep the fans interested. Fans who had once been willing to watch a young and growing team were proving to have far less patience for an underachieving bunch of high-priced players, especially after the newer expansion Diamondbacks already captured their World Series title. Mike Hampton was traded following the 2002 season, yet Colorado continued to pay part of his salary. In 2002, the Rockies finished eight games under .500. They finished seven under in 2003, behind Bell's replacement, Manager Clint Hurdle.

Shea Stadium
Colorado Rockies @ New York Mets
May 11, 2002
Section 4, Row Q, Seat 8

My last two stops in May were both in New York, to see the Mets and the Yankees. New York has an intricate baseball history, one that began long before the advent of professional baseball. When the National League was founded in 1876, the New York Giants and the Brooklyn Trolley Dodgers were founding members. In 1903, New York businessmen purchased the original Baltimore Orioles and moved the team to New York, where they would play as the American League's Highlanders. The Highlanders had a decade of success, and in 1913 they moved from Hilltop Park to the Polo Grounds, which they shared with the Giants. They also adopted a new team name: the New York Yankees. For years the three teams shared fierce rivalries, and in the 1940s and 1950s it was not unusual to see one if not two of them playing for the World Championship.

Following the 1957 season, Walter O'Malley, the owner of the Brooklyn Dodgers, decided he needed a new stadium in a better part of Brooklyn. Robert Moses, the parks commissioner of the city, refused to allow O'Malley to buy the land that he wanted. Moses wanted to build a city-owned park in Flushing, Queens, and move the team out of Brooklyn. Neither satisfied with that option nor able to buy the desired land himself, O'Malley realized that he could get the city of Los Angeles to build him a stadium if he moved the team to the West Coast. He and the owner of the Giants, Horace Stoneham, teamed up to convince the other owners that the West Coast was a viable option. Suddenly, only the Yankees remained in New York—as well as thousands of broken-hearted fans.

In 1959, the Continental Baseball League was formed to compete with the American and National Leagues. To ward off the contender, the two older leagues agreed to expand, swallowing several of the proposed Continental ownership groups. This marked the first MLB expansion since its inception. The New York Mets were granted a National League franchise, which would begin play in 1962. The Mets adopted the colors of the previous teams in order to attract fans, and they quickly filled the void the departed NL teams had left.

The Mets play at Shea Stadium, one of the first of the multi-purpose stadiums to be built in the 1960s. Shea is located in Flushing, Queens, where Robert Moses had wanted O'Malley to relocate his stadium. In the early days, the Mets shared Shea with the Jets of the American Football Conference. The seats are color coded by level, and the brilliant hues add to the sensory experience. However, one could never accuse Shea of having an abundance of atmosphere. It is a giant place, and when one isn't down on field level, one feels very far away from the action. Because Shea was built to accommodate football as well, the seats in the outfield are poorly angled for baseball. Even though corporate ticket holders own most of those seats, they barely afford a view of the batter. Both the mezzanine and loge provide better views of the game.

During the 2002 season, Fred Wilpon, part owner of the Mets for twenty-two years, bought his partner's shares and became sole owner of the team. The city of New York had agreed to help build both New York teams new stadiums prior to the events of September 11, 2001. Following that day, however, it seemed unlikely that any new stadiums would be built anytime soon, unless they would somehow be connected to the 2012 Olympic bid. With a new stadium now out of the question, Mets ownership decided to spruce up Shea in the 2002 off-season, painting the concourses, re-carpeting the luxury boxes, and adding a photo montage to the balcony of the loge section. The montage is an attractive feature designed to remind troubled Mets fans of the club's past glories.

Shea Stadium could possibly be the loudest stadium in professional baseball. Its sound system is not very good, which may be why everything seems like it's being played at top volume. It is always noisy between at-bats and innings. The in-game entertainment is merely filler to occupy dead space, and it does little to add to the baseball experience. I must admit, there are traditions in Shea that I would hate to see them do away with, including the playing of "Crazy Mary," an Italian novelty song that normally concludes the seventh-inning stretch.

One legitimate reason for playing the music so loudly at Shea, maybe to match the noise made by the airplanes that fly overhead en route to nearby La Guardia Airport. I always thought the noise of the jets added something special to the stadium, sort of a "tenth man" effect. So prevalent was the noise that the Mets even used airplanes in their video "races" between innings, the ones where fans cheer for the animated character that corresponds with their section. These races may seem irrelevant to baseball, but as I traveled I found that the games changed to be relevant to the city in which they were being played (i.e. jet skis in Florida, snow boarders in Denver). Though the games are another way advertising has crept into the national pastime, they did provide a connection to each particular locale. To make it more relevant to the fans, though, the characters in the races should actually reflect the reactions in the stands. Noise meters could be placed in sections of the stands, allowing the results of the readings to determine the results of the race on the jumbotron. If the loudest fans are in the upper deck then the plane, train or mountain biker representing them would win. This would carry over the spirit of competition from the field to the stands and instill a different kind of ownership for the fans, as well as create a sense of pride for season ticket holders in those areas. The fans would also become actively engaged with the sponsor creating more value on that front. Connecting the fans to the experience at the ballpark should be the goal. Teams might even be able to reward the season ticket holders in the season-winning area, and in this way, reward them for cheering for their team.

The Mets have other in-game entertainment that draws in the fans. In 2002, they had fan favorite John Franco, who was out for the season, make an appearance on the screen during each game with a trivia question. This was a great idea. Though any player could have been used to a similar effect, Franco, a New York boy, held a special place in Mets fans hearts, and it was nice for them to be able to connect to him in some way while he was out for the season. This is the right type of on-screen entertainment, the kind that educates the fans and promotes the team as a group.

New York fans may not be the most vocal fans, but they are perhaps the most faithful. Among the four teams that have played in one of the five boroughs of New York—Giants, Dodgers, Yankees, Mets—at least one has appeared in more than half of the World Championship Series that have been played. That is to say that out of 100 World Series' that have been played, New York has been represented in 53 of them. No matter which team you are rooting for, winning seems to be a part of New York.

New York fans may also be the most knowledgeable. They follow baseball closely and understand its nuances. The guy sitting next to me had been watching baseball for forty years. He could tell me who was on the team that won the World Series twenty years ago *and* who was on the team five years later that finished under .500. The woman in front of me had come to games as a little girl and learned to keep score. Each fan knew how each player had been acquired, be it trade, free agency, or, the prized homegrown player. And in the case of a trade, they knew how well the traded player did with his next team. Paul O'Neil was a Yankee favorite not only because of his drive and competitiveness but also because he turned out to be so much better than Roberto Kelley, the player the Yankees gave up to acquire him. George Bassil, a Mets fan, told me about a pitcher who was once asked how he knew the fans in New York were the most knowledgeable. His reply: "Once you have heard 25,000 people call a balk on you, you know."

Yankee Stadium
Seattle Mariners @ New York Yankees
May 3, 2002
Box 274, Row E, Seat 4

The Yankees, the last team from May, are the most prominent team of the past century, winning twenty-six of the one hundred World Series and appearing thirty-nine times. Next behind them is the Dodgers, appearing eighteen times and winning only six. The franchise's history is incomparable to any other.

It is difficult to figure out exactly why their fan base is so huge. Is it because they have been so successful, or is it because they have the largest metropolitan area on which to draw? The incomparable success rate certainly cannot be taken lightly. Regardless, the reality is that the Yankees are a successful and popular team, one whose enormous fan base allows them to spend more money than any other club. Yankees President Randy Levine said during a press conference in December 2002, "The Yankees are about winning." There is no doubt that winning will trump any other factor in creating new fans.

The heroes of the Yankees are intricately connected to our popular culture. The great figures of the Yankees are part of the American lexicon. Babe Ruth, Lou Gehrig, Joe DiMaggio, Yogi Berra, Mickey Mantle, Billy Martin, Thurmon Munson, and Reggie Jackson are all men that mean more to us than just baseball. Some represent excesses, some hard work, others raw talent, self-confidence, humility, and tragedy. Entering Yankee Stadium is unlike entering any other ballpark, because our history is laid out there in front of us, from Monument Park in the outfield to the short porch down the right field line. So many of our shared experiences have played themselves out in Yankee Stadium—often during the televised "games of the week,"—that we all feel a connection to the place in some way. The Yankees also remind us of this history at every opportunity, for example, by playing biographies on select Yankees on the Jumbotron prior to each home game.

I happened to attend a series against Seattle, a popular series in New York due to the success that the Mariners have had over the past few years. I didn't expect to see many Seattle fans in the stands for two very important reasons. First, Seattle is located 3000 miles away. It is very hard for an Easterner to follow a West Coast team, since home games don't begin until 10 P.M. Eastern Standard Time. There isn't any coverage on local news programs of these games unless the local team is playing there. Second, the Mariner's didn't come into existence until 1977, seventy-four years after the Yankees and fifteen years after the Mets. It would be hard to imagine a native New Yorker choosing to follow the Mariners, yet there were a few at the game, mostly young teens whose fathers had taken them to see Ken Griffey Jr. play during his prime, when they were just boys. Even though Junior was no longer there, the success of the Seattle franchise had kept them interested. There were also a few natives of Washington, who had made the trip to New York for the dual purpose of dropping a few tourist dollars and seeing their M's play.

Yankee Stadium, built in 1923, was the first athletic facility in the United States to be referred to as a stadium. It isn't very comfortable, as the original seats are too small for the average person. They are angled properly, however, and with the exception of the upper deck in the outfield, you can see everything relatively well.

The Yankees have the marketing thing worked out well. Yankee merchandise is plentiful not only in the stadium but in just about every facility in the league and in shops around the world. Michael Kay, a Yankees announcer with the Yes Network, became known for describing the Yankee uniform on the radio, emphasizing the "interlocking NY" on the cap. It is such a familiar image that kids the world over can draw up the mental picture immediately. It's such a ubiquitous image in New York, in fact, that it is hard to find a person who doesn't own some piece of Yankees apparel.

Do the Yankees do everything right in terms of the fan experience? No. The stadium concourse is dank, dark, and cold. They have blocked up all views of the area surrounding the stadium except for a small patch down the right field line. They have managed to keep low-end ticket prices down over these past few successful years, but the field seat prices have risen dramatically. The Yankees, however, see no need to rush to fix any of this as long as they keep winning—and as long as they continue to play in the most celebrated stadium in baseball. The history and the championships make it easy to suffer through the mild discomforts. Yankee Stadium live, with all its excited fans and their enthusiastic cheering, is a unique experience. It is well worth leaving our cozy living rooms and shelling out the money for it. Our connection to its history and to its fans, who love the game so much, will keep us coming again and again.

3

Sluggers, Gloves, and Good Eyes

It is the heroes of our youth who create the magic of baseball for us. For me, the Reds in the 1970s were an amazing collection of players. Though Johnny Bench and Pete Rose were the superstars of that team, neither was my favorite. That honor goes to Dave Concepcion. He won the NL Gold Glove five times, including four straight from 1974 to 1977. I loved his grace and agility, and I'm still a sucker for a beautifully-turned double play. The name Concepcion also seemed quite exotic to a little girl from Ohio. I learned later that he was the first big leaguer from Venezuela, a country that now boasts such stars as Omar Vizquel, Freddy Garcia, Andres Galarraga, and Ozzie Guillen.

Billy Hatcher, John Franco, Todd Walker, and all the other former Reds all hold a special place in my heart. Well, that's not quite true. Upon moving to NYC, I encountered a trove of fans that still rued the day Tom Seaver was traded to the Reds, and I did too. "Tom Terrific," as he was called, is one of the few Reds that I could never seem to get behind. My friend Tom Kelly, a rabid Mets fan, told me, "As a boy, I pinned all of my hopes and dreams of the Mets winning a World Series on Seaver. And he made those dreams come true" (by helping the Mets win a Championship in 1969 and another pennant in 1973). "I'll always love him," he added. I, too, pinned all my hopes and dreams on Mr. Seaver when he arrived in Cincinnati in mid-1977, but *my* dreams didn't come true. The Dodgers were already too far ahead in the NL West, and Don Gullett, another Reds hero, was playing with the much-hated Yankees. Seaver pitched a no-hitter in 1978 and, with the exception of his final year in Cincinnati, never had an ERA higher than 3.64, but he never led us to the pennant. As an adult, I understand that it takes more than one good pitcher to get to the World Series, and this was especially true in Seaver's case, since his arrival coincided with the breakup of the Big Red Machine. But as a nine-year-old, my disappointment rested completely on the shoulders of number 41. Since Mr. Seaver is beloved by so many, I doubt if he'll mind me holding on to that disappointment all these years later.

By the end of the 1970s, the Big Red machine was gone. In 1977, Tony Perez was traded, and in 1979 Pete Rose became a free agent and went to Philly for big money. It would be nearly twenty years before I could forgive Rose, realizing that baseball is a business and that he did what any sensible person would have done. (Although I also have recollections of headlines about his divorce and a mistress, which added to my distaste for him.) In the middle of the 1981 season, the Major League Baseball Player's Association (MLBPA) went on strike. Baseball was cancelled for fifty-two days. The season would continue, but I, a teenager at the time, had lost my interest. The momentum of the season had ended, and by the time the game returned, I was thinking about school instead of worrying about which teams were going to get playoff berths. That was the beginning of my first break with baseball.

Pete Rose helped the Phillies to two pennants and one World Series Championship, and after a short stint in Montreal, he returned to the Reds as the prodigal son. He was a great player-manager, and during this stint he broke Ty Cobb's record for base hits, a record that had stood for almost sixty years. That day was one of the greatest in Reds' history, but I did not fully appreciate it, as baseball had begun to take a back seat to my own activities.

In 1988, Concepcion finally retired, having played his entire nineteen-year career as a Red. Barry Larkin would replace him and, following Concepcion's example, would play his entire career for the Reds.

In 1989, Rose was investigated for gambling, the only activity specifically banned in a major-league player's contract. In exchange for a quick closure of the investigation, he accepted a lifetime ban from the game, though he always maintained his innocence. Many people in Cincinnati took the investigation personally. Rose was, after all, a hometown kid who on several occasions had turned the world's attention to Cincinnati and had managed to make the Queen City a contender again. For many, the pride he had brought the town on those occasions outweighed his bad behavior off the field. As for me, I was still upset at him for leaving the Reds to go to Philly, so I was okay with him being sent away again.

In 1990, Lou Piniella was named the new manager of the Reds. Fortunately, he was able to build on the success of the Rose years. The Reds beat a talented Pirates team for the pennant, and then they defeated the heavily favored Oakland A's in the World Series. In my travels for this book, both Mike Gallego and Mike Bordick, members of that A's team, reminded me with more than a little bitterness that the Reds "weren't supposed to win that World Series."

I had finished college by this point and was living in the East, but the success of the Reds drew me back into baseball and filled me with nostalgia for my hometown. Ken Griffey (by then labeled Senior) was the only member of the Big Red Machine still on a major-league roster, in Seattle. It was time for new heroes to capture the imagination of kids in southern Ohio.

Sometimes it's the player's charismatic smile as he poses for a press photo, like that of Dwight Gooden, or the way he runs to first when he could have walked, like Enos Slaughter, Pete Rose, or David Eckstein. It might be the way he bashes home runs, like Mickey Mantle or Mark McGwire. It might be that he just seems like "good people," like Jim Thome, or that we wore his number when we played little league. Or it might be our presence at a great moment in the sport that will forever make us love one particular guy and the team he represents.

In baseball, any guy on the team can have his own group of fans, and he doesn't have to be the star. When I was in Anaheim and St. Louis I saw fans wearing the numbers and names of just about every player on the field. Other fans reminded me of players that had slipped from the forefront of my own memory, such as Dave Martinez and Richie Ashburn. I now believe that there are few players who aren't held in special regard by someone, somewhere. I met a young guy, drinking beer across from Edison Field in Anaheim, who had grown up a Dodgers fan because his little league team had been the Dodgers. His favorite player had been Graig Nettles. Raymond Green, a self-proclaimed Mets fan, described wanting to be a third baseman because of Nettles and even creating a game named after him. The game went something like this: one kid would hit ground balls to the others, and whoever made the most incredible catch, while committing the fewest errors, won. Tim Richardson talked about growing up in South Central L.A., where Dodger games were an "unimaginable treat." He watched the games on television with his cousin and later they would "go out to the run-down sandlot to imagine [they] were Maury Wills, Sandy Koufax, or Don Drysdale."

Jim Kriedler, a Phillies fan, thought the term "tailor-made double play" was coined in honor of his favorite second baseman, Tony Taylor. Jim started as a second baseman in little league and wore number 8, just like Taylor. There was a little boy who sat behind me in St. Louis who wanted to know if J. D. Drew was the best outfielder in the world. He liked Drew because they both shared the same number 7—Drew for the Cardinals, the boy for his little league squad. Tom Howard grew up in Los Angeles in a family of Dodger fans. He was a left-handed first baseman on his little league team. In 1986, the Angels brought up Wally Joyner to play first, and suddenly Tom had a left-handed first baseman to study. "He quickly became my favorite player, and I grew to love the Angels more and more every year after that," he wrote.

Sometimes it's not exactly a favorite player that draws us in, but rather a memory of greatness. I think of the businessmen who sat in front of me in Atlanta, who were excited to tell not only *me* about some of their great Braves memories but also each other. Tom Malady saw Hank Aaron break Babe Ruth's total homerun record on television, but it was a powerful experience nevertheless. I was in Chicago the summer Barry Bonds hit his 600th home run. The White Sox game had ended, and I was sitting in the hotel bar, doing my notes and watching the Giants game on television. Around the corner of the bar, also unwinding from the game, were Arthur Rhodes and Jeff Nelson, then of the Mariners. We all sat there just watching, amazed at the feat and then dumbstruck at the brawl that followed, a giant scrum to retrieve the ball. That moment, even though I experienced it through television, will always be vivid in my mind.

Great catches capture people's imagination, too. I heard a boy outside PNC Park ask his father if the amazing diving catch that Brian Giles had made to end the Pirates/Marlins game was the greatest catch he had ever seen. I, too, thought it was an amazing catch. Hopefully, it will remain in that boy's memory for a long time.

Other people associate their love of baseball with general memories of players playing the game. Red Sox fan Brian Dunham fondly reflected on seeing George Scott "hitting them out of Fenway," and being allowed to stay up late to see Carlton Fisk's famous game-six home run. James Harris remembers looking in the paper on the day he was to attend his first game and "jumping for joy when [he] learned that Juan Marichal was pitching." A Houston fan told me that he had been named after Bobby Thomson because his father had watched the famed "shot heard round the world" while his wife was in labor.

I met a man in Milwaukee who was visiting from Los Angeles. He had become a Dodger fan when he was in school, and his teacher had taken his class to the library and told them each to select a book. He had found one about Jackie Robinson. Though Robinson wasn't playing anymore (this would have been the mid-1970s), the story of Robinson breaking the color barrier touched the young boy so much that he not only learned about Robinson but also studied baseball in general, and especially the Dodgers.

Personal interactions often cement the bond a person has for a particular player or team. Ray Amico told me how he attended his first game with his neighbor, a friend of the Mets management. The two were sitting in the first row next to the dugout. "During the game, Tom Seaver was in the dugout, right next to where I was sitting. I said, 'Mr. Seaver, Mr. Seaver! Would you sign this picture?' but he was about to go out to the mound. He looked over and shook my hand and went onto the field. From that day on, I was not only a Mets fan; I was a National League fan and a huge Tom Seaver fan." Maybe I would feel differently about Seaver if I, too, had gotten to shake his hand as a kid.

At an Indians game, I met a man wearing a Mets t-shirt who was sitting with his friends in their Ohio sports garb. The young fellow from Ohio told me the following story. When he was young, he opened a pack of baseball cards and discovered a picture of Dwight Gooden. He immediately liked the way "Doc" looked, so he pulled that card out and poured over his stats on the back. He quickly became obsessed with the Mets, and when his family took a vacation to Florida during spring training, his dad tried to get tickets to one of the Mets spring-training home games. Unfortunately, even then Mets games were highly popular, most likely due to the large numbers of New Yorkers who had relocated South. All of the Mets home games were sold out. His family then planned a trip to see the Mets play at the Phillies' spring training facility. Prior to the game, the kids and their mom were walking around, and they spotted a young Darryl Strawberry in the outfield sitting on a bench with a towel around his neck. The kids went over to say hello and to share their disappointment, having found out that Strawberry would not be playing that day. Strawberry said he would be playing the next day at home and suggested that they come to see that game. The kids explained that the game was already sold out and that they wouldn't be able to do that. Strawberry asked them how many tickets they needed and then told them the tickets would be waiting for them. The boys were elated, but their mom, who was a little skeptical, went to find their father, who returned and questioned Darryl further.

"It's a two-hour drive. Are you sure you can leave us tickets?"

There will be tickets waiting he was told. The next day, not only were four tickets waiting, but also they were also located in the players' family section, their mom sitting next to Lenny Dykstra's wife throughout the game. From then on, this young Ohio boy was a Mets fan. Strawberry's much-publicized drug problems in later years haven't diminished the affection that he and others feel for the star batter. When I hear stories like this, it is clear why he has been given so many chances. What would happen if each player in MLB picked out one kid and his family and gave them his tickets for a game?

Teams often work with local boys and girls clubs to give kids the opportunity to see a game. Players, though, don't have a direct impact on this act of charity. By offering tickets directly to families every now and then, they might be able to strengthen their connections to the fans and the community, which can only enhance their 'team' experience. Though the possibility they will be traded always exists, the players gaining an opportunity to understand those in the stands can be a rewarding experience for them both on and off the field.

There were quite a few people whom I met in 2002 whose love of the sport was actually diminished because of their interactions with players. One man told me about the time his five-year-old son approached a Dodgers outfielder for an autograph while the player waited alone in the lobby for an elevator. The player looked at the kid and said he "didn't have time." The little boy retreated back across the lobby to his father's side and watched as the outfielder stood waiting for the elevator for a couple more minutes. One former Baltimore outfielder, upon my being introduced to him as someone writing a book about fans, said, "Fans are rude." I watched a Mariners outfielder walk by a stream of autograph seekers outside his hotel without even acknowledging their requests. Moments earlier, Lou Piniella had stopped to give a signature to each one.

Craig Biggio, after going one for four with a walk against the Cubs at Wrigley, returned to his hotel with a few other members of the Astros. A family was waiting in the lobby, and as he entered the kids excitedly ran up to him so he could sign their baseballs. One boy piped up, "Mr. Biggio, you were great today!" The second baseman explained that he would be happy to sign anything until the elevator came, but that he would then have to go. As he returned the final ball he would sign that day, the elevator doors opened. The father then asked for a quick picture with the boys. Biggio agreed, though he said it would have to be quick. The father messed with the camera as the other players and I got into the elevator and held the door for him. After a lot of fumbling, the father took the photo and Biggio joined us. When the elevator doors closed, he relaxed against the wall and heaved a deep sigh. He hadn't had a great night on the field, and hearing the kids compliment him on his play probably didn't make him feel any better. His generosity of spirit made permanent Astros fans out of those kids, though, even if Biggio didn't realize it at the time. As Brian Dunham explained, "When players hustle and are friendly to the kids, it makes a difference."

What these stories have in common is that they demonstrate the value we place on our connections to the players. For most it is not the autograph that they will cherish, though it will serve as a lasting reminder of their experience. Had that Dodger outfielder, or any of the others who were too tired to sign an autograph, simply looked at the kid and said, "I'm sorry, I can't right now, but I hope to see you at the game," the fan would have gone away happy. The problem is that halfway through a grueling summer, players often forget that it is not really the autograph that people are seeking. Maybe they never even knew it in the first place. It is the connection the fans make, both to their fame and also to their talent. Tom Seaver simply shook Ray Amico's hand and created an invaluable memory. Misti Potter from Alabama told me, "When teams throw the baseballs into the stands, or when a player hands a child a ball, that makes it all worthwhile."

Players, too, have something to gain from interactions with the average fan. Mark McGwire said during his home run race of 1998, "It's amazing that a guy that swings a bat can affect the country." The emotion that he showed upon breaking Roger Maris's record, which had stood for thirty-seven years, was certainly maximized by the expression of joy that came from the fans in the stands and on the field that night. You do not need to be an amazing athlete—or any kind of celebrity, for that matter—to make a difference in people's lives, but certainly the stature of the professional sportsman makes even small gestures extra special. The wiggle of a kid's hat creates more affection for baseball than any signature alone ever could. Both on and off the field, the most valuable thing we can give each other is respect.

Disrespectful fans, however, seem to have spoiled the players' impressions of the people sitting in the stands. On September 19, 2002, people attending the Royals vs. White Sox game at Comiskey witnessed a terrible sight. A father and son in the stands ran onto the field in the ninth inning and began punching Kansas City's first base coach, Tom Gamboa. Luckily, the players on the bench reacted quickly, and luckily their dugout was on the first-base side. They came out, tackled the perpetrators, and pulled them off until security could arrive. It was frightening to watch on television—I can imagine it must have been even scarier to witness such a thing from the stands.

During one game of the 2002 World Series in Anaheim, several fans sitting in the front row of the right-field stands felt that it was their duty to help the Angels by hitting the Giants right fielder with red CheerStix while he tried to retrieve a ball hit deep into the corner. With a repeat of the White Sox incident occurring in April 2003, and other fans running onto the field regularly, it has become a scary time to be a baseball player. Though none of these people represent baseball's real fans, these events set the tone that exists in players' minds.

In Montreal during the 2002 season, the Atlanta Braves stayed in a hotel where the bar opens onto the lobby. After the game, several players gathered together to have a bite to eat, relax, and even play a little pool. About fifty people stood around outside the lounge, staring in at the team. Every now and then, one fan would work up the courage to walk in and ask Chipper Jones or Javy Lopez for their autograph, and the players would comply. I'm not sure the fans ever took the time to take a look around and imagine what it must be like to go through that eighty days a year. The Braves had similar problems in each city where I saw them play. Just as players can benefit from reaching out to fans, the fans should treat the athletes with respect and courtesy. The perception exists among players that fans only like them (or any celebrity) as long as they can get something from them. Connecting with a player by telling him how much he means to you personally might prove more rewarding for both of you than simply asking for an autograph. Players on the field give us positive memories; when we ask for their time, we should be willing to give something back as well. When the fan-athlete relationship is based on mutual respect, all of the parties reap greater benefits.

Players indeed make a lot of money to play the game, but we need to understand what it takes to play it at the level that they do. We see them stand around during batting practice, move into the cage, take a few swings, and then retreat to the clubhouse. A couple will stand on the base paths and catch a few balls. The guys in the outfield seem to be socializing. Then they play a game, where they do a lot of standing around (except for the pitcher and catcher) and occasionally steal the show with an amazing play. The reality is that for a 7:00 P.M. game, they have to be on the field by 5:00 P.M. for batting practice. Prior to that, batters need to look at scouting reports on the pitchers they will face, review video tape of their previous at-bats, visit the trainer for treatment of the aches and pains that come with being a thirty-year-old athlete, and get into uniform. Pitchers need to meet with their catchers and pitching coaches to review the reports on the twenty-five men on the opposing teams and come up with a strategy for pitching to each of them. A pitcher usually arrives at the park by 2:00 P.M. for a 7:00 P.M. game and coaches arrive an hour or two before that. By the time the game is over and the hurlers have thrown a hundred or more pitches—at speeds we don't even drive at—they have been at the park for at least nine hours. By the time they return to the hotel, eat, and unwind, it's two in the morning. If there is a day game after a night game, they will have to be back at the park by 9 A.M. Every third day, they find themselves in a new city and a new park, with new ground rules. They stay in nice hotels and travel on private planes, but the schedule is tough. I did it for one summer; however, I was fortunate enough not to have to stand in the outfield on my toes during a three-and-a-half-hour game while people screamed at me that I sucked.

The schedule does not excuse bad behavior on the part of players, however. Unfortunately, the young players coming up today were rarely the kids we see in the stands hoping a big leaguer will talk to them. They were all busy playing little league, perfecting their craft, even at the young ages of nine and ten. They don't understand the importance of that connection. Generating new fans should be part of their job, and the players who do it well should be rewarded. Players need to understand that we, the paying customers, are baseball's driving engine, and that their salaries depend on us.

Prior to the advent of free agency, only the best players were able to support themselves by baseball alone. To supplement their income, players would earn money by making public appearances for the club and for local businesses, as well as by working at various jobs during the off-season. With the advent of baseball card shows, players could make additional money autographing baseball memorabilia. Veteran players today, if they manage their money well, have no need to concern themselves with these extras, yet the club still pays them additional money for making personal appearances on its behalf. This is germane to the whole problem. Players need to realize that they are the ultimate beneficiaries of these appearances. For each connection they make, one more fan is going to bring his or her family to the stadium. If more tickets are sold, the club can spend more on players, and more money spent on good players can result in a better team.

Clubs should make this a prominent issue in future collective bargaining agreements. Imagine the publicity that would be generated if each player were required in his contract to make three to four personal appearances a year on behalf of the club. Imagine the benefits to the surrounding communities that these appearances would have, a concern raised by several fans, including Brian Carlson. It is no coincidence that Pete Rose's greatest group of supporters comes from the communities around Cincinnati. During his prime, the Reds were great benefactors to the community, and Pete, being a hometown kid, created a lot of pride by bringing attention to southern Ohio. These efforts allow teams in small markets to survive, and they will continue to do so in the future.

MLB has decided to limit the amount of debt a club can carry in relation to its assets. This limit will make it more important that each team spends its money wisely, and it should get players to take a greater interest in helping their franchise grow. If the team can earn more profits by increasing fan interest and advertising revenues, it will be able to continue giving out large player contracts.

Today, a portion of the money earned from the sale of MLB merchandise goes into a pool shared by players. What if that portion were decreased by a small amount and more money went to players who sold the most jerseys with their names on them? The individual player might then see a direct correlation between the size of his paycheck and the extent to which he reaches out to the fans. If players can see financial repercussions, there would be another reason for them to learn the value of the fans.

Players establishing personal connections with fans might also make fans more interested in the issues discussed during labor talks. James, a Mets fan, said, "Half of these spoiled millionaire players [don't sign] autographs and then [they] act like they are working men like you and me and deserve the fans' support against management." That thought echoed throughout the country in 2002 as labor negotiations dragged on. Players seem to have become less interested in establishing personal relationships with fans in recent years, and fans have become accordingly less tolerant of players' complaints. The reality is that no worker anywhere would refuse millions of dollars to do his or her job, if that kind of money were offered. But baseball is the sport of the common man, and the common man feels that he's lost the ability to identify with the players. Since average people don't often have the opportunity to see athletes do anything but extraordinary feats, they don't understand that they too have ordinary problems. Ray Amico, also a Mets fan, pointed out, "I've never sided with the owners on anything. I don't root for them; I root for the players on the field. [The owners] have a right to make profits, and not to be handcuffed by an increasing expense structure that winds up running up the cost of everything to the fans." During the labor agreement talks in 2002, Vance Wilson, assistant players rep for the New York Mets, said, "We need to spend time with the fans to let them know they are important."[8] Players need to get back on the winning side of the public relations war, but they can only do that by reaching out and embracing the people who buy the tickets.

Teams must also reach out to the players to maximize the effect that stars can have on attendance. By promoting players, whether or not their long-term plans include them, clubs can reap the rewards that talented athletes can produce as members of the public-relations team. Alex Rodriguez, who played for the Texas Rangers in 2002, went on record, saying that "it's time for the owners and players to come together like the NBA does and start promoting their players…For some reason, when people talk about players, they say this guy is good, but not for that money. They have been enemies so long we're losing the wars."[9] Dick Young, writing in the April 12, 1969, issue of the *Sporting News*, said, "Performance and publicity make superstars. A Roberto Clemente would have been a superstar with the proper buildup. Baseball did very little for Roberto Clemente, and now it's too late."[10] Owners and players need to respect and trust each other in order to take full advantage of the assets that they possess.

If we put the onus on pro athletes to act as representatives of their clubs, are we also asking them to be role models? In reality, we can't ever expect anyone to act as a role model. Both fans and athletes, though, need to examine their behavior on a daily basis and make an effort to represent themselves in a manner that will make each proud of their relationship to the other. At one time, I felt that John Rocker's racist and homophobic comments to a *Sports Illustrated* reporter in 2000 reflected poorly on his team, the Atlanta Braves. In some ways I still do, since the Braves made no effort to discipline him or to separate themselves from his controversial statements, as CBS did when Andy Rooney made controversial statements about female reporters on the sidelines at NFL games, or as the Rockies did when pitcher Todd Jones made homophobic comments to the press at the start of the 2003 season.

Everyone has the right to his or her opinion and the right to express that opinion. For each young adult, be they fans in Chicago or star athletes in Atlanta, understanding that one's actions have an effect on others is a hard lesson. It is only through this understanding, though, that any of us can be role models.

I have learned a lot from baseball players. When I was six, Carlton Fisk taught me that if you want it bad enough, you could will anything to happen. In 2002, Craig Biggio taught me the importance of being gracious, no matter how tired you are. I have finally forgiven Pete Rose for going to Philly. I learned two things from him: first, to hustle, always; second, only games can be perfect—people never are. Since his gambling problem was exposed, we as a country have witnessed many of our "heroes" fall. Darryl Strawberry has gone to jail several times while struggling with drug addiction. Jayson Williams, the former NBA player, shot his chauffeur and seemed to try to cover it up. Catholic priests have been accused of molesting young boys, and Presidents Clinton and Kennedy have both been exposed for having affairs with interns less than half their age.

We have learned to judge presidents by what they accomplished during their terms. Why can't we look at athletes the same way? Pete Rose, with all his hits, is a big part of why I love baseball. Does it really matter that he and others like him aren't the men we imagine them to be? He may have hurt baseball in his later years, but no more than he helped it when I was a kid. We can try to learn from athletes' positive contributions to society, but, perhaps, we can also learn from their mistakes.

4

Circling the Bases: Part II

SkyDome
Tampa Bay Devil Rays @ Toronto Blue Jays
June 5, 2002
Aisle 127, Row 3, Seat 108

In the beginning of June, I headed off for a three-city trip beginning with a first visit to Toronto. It would be the second time I saw the Blue Jays on my tour of the league, since I had seen them play in Tampa Bay. The Blue Jays began as an expansion team in 1977, the same year as the Seattle Mariners. On August 9 of that first year, the Blue Jays passed the 1 million mark in attendance, setting the record for a first-year expansion team. By the end of 1979, the Jays would hold the record for highest home attendance by an expansion team in its first three years of play, with 4,695,288 tickets sold.

After playing for thirteen years at Exhibition Stadium, the Blue Jays moved to the Toronto SkyDome in the middle of the 1989 season, where they would set the record for single-season attendance at just over 4 million. There, in the first baseball stadium built with a retractable roof, the team gained sole possession of first place in its division for the first time since 1985. The Jays headed to their first World Series in 1992, beating the Atlanta Braves. The following year, they were able to repeat as champions with the help of John Olerud, Roberto Alomar, and Paul Molitor, who finished one, two, and three in the batting race. That series, against the Phillies, ended in the sixth game when Joe Carter hit the game-winning home run.

The success didn't last, however, and beginning in 1996, attendance has declined each season through 2001, when they sold a mere 1,895,547 tickets. Though the Jays had won two World Series in the past ten years, the perennial dominance of the Yankees and the Red Sox in their division have made filling the stadium difficult.

The meager crowd in the stands on my first night in Toronto hardly outnumbered those I had seen in Tampa Bay. The fans in Toronto who arrived in time for batting practice headed right to their seats. Few people stood on the edge of the field hoping for a ball. It was difficult to find fans who seemed enthusiastic about the team. The several ushers I spoke to felt the same. Although they seemed to like watching the team, they found it hard to get excited about them these days. The Blue Jays were gaining a reputation for trading away their best players to offset skyrocketing salaries without a clear vision of who would replace them. The Yankees' ability to continue to dole out high salaries didn't help matters, and things would only get worse when Raul Mondesi was traded to the Bronx Bombers a few weeks after my visit. Eric Hinske, a young third basemen, was one shining spot in 2002, but he wasn't enough to bring the fans back to the SkyDome.

During the game, I sat next to a young woman, Jennifer, who had grown up in the area but now lived in Vancouver. Her grandmother was a huge Blue Jays fan, and Jennifer's memories of the team were tied to special memories of her grandmother. Behind me sat a gentleman who was a women's fast-pitch softball coach. He was very fond of the game, but not as fond of the Blue Jays as he once had been. He said that he didn't see any evidence of the "love of the game" in the players on the field, and that he preferred the enthusiasm of the young women whom he coached. Both of these people had watched baseball in Toronto avidly from their first season through the two World Series victories, but the strike of 1994 had damaged their view of professional baseball. They rarely come to games anymore, and they don't follow the team closely.

The SkyDome is unique in several respects. The outfield wall is actually formed by a hotel and restaurants, which were built adjacent to the stadium to afford a view of the action. The dome was built to accommodate a sometimes-hostile climate in Toronto, so the SkyDome has an Astroturf field. Though there is dirt around the actual bases, the rest of the field resembles a dark green carpet. The Blue Jays do not open their stadium for home team batting practice, but I was able to watch from the restaurant overlooking the field. On this night, the dome was closed due to the chance of rain. From where I sat in the restaurant, I could see the Jays hitting and fielding, and I quickly took note of the difference Astroturf makes. Unlike the plush turf at Tropicana Field in Tampa, the Jays' turf was hard and the ball moved quickly, with no blades of grass to slow it down. My 1970s Reds had also played on artificial turf, but I had been away from Riverfront for so long I had forgotten how fast the ball moved on it. Perhaps the open sky of Riverfront had allowed me to overlook the nuances of baseball played on artificial turf. In the SkyDome, however, the differences were stark. With its closed roof reverberating hollow echoes of balls being hit and vendors hawking their goods, the stadium seemed much more like a high school gymnasium during indoor softball practice than a traditional baseball field.

The SkyDome is loud even with only about 15,000 people inside. Even though the cheers were sparse there, the echoes could cause anyone to get a headache over a three-hour game. Perhaps because of this, the Jays seem to have the least in-game entertainment, choosing subtle ways to fill the time between innings. The people sitting around me complained about the few activities that did occur, seeing them as little more than crass commercialism; however, compared to the other stadiums I visited, the SkyDome was admirably quiet. This sensitivity to commercialization might help explain why there were so few people chasing balls and seeking autographs during B.P. The local rooters I met clearly appreciated the contributions of Mondesi, Delgado, and Hinske, but they didn't seem to need apparel bearing their names in order to feel a connection with them. What they did desire was for the players to show that they cared—by playing hard every night and winning games.

The Blue Jays don't suffer from the same lack of merchandising as the Marlins. Despite limited concession space, there were vendors everywhere, all with a different array of merchandise so that you needed to visit more than one booth to see everything they had to offer, including a collection of unique autographed memorabilia. Only teams like the Braves, Giants and the Yankees, with their large fan bases and successes on the field, matched the Jays in the amount of merchandise available in their stadiums.

My second game was on the first Thursday in June, which is traditionally when all the schools in Toronto load the fifth- and sixth-grade students onto buses and take them to a Blue Jays game. Today the opened dome stadium was nearly sold out, full of kids who had escaped classes for the day. The concourses, which I had thought easy to move through the day before, were packed with exuberant pre-teens. As these were not typical Jays fans wandering about, I made my way to my seat early.

Once there, I met a great baseball fan, who had been a season ticket holder since the franchise was founded, and his seven-year-old granddaughter, Molly. Prior to following the Blue Jays he had been a Tigers' fan, since Detroit was just a few hours away. He had a program autographed by Hank Greenberg from the 1945 World Series along with other memorabilia from seasons past. He shared stories with me of great players whom he had seen at both Tiger and Yankee Stadiums. Every so often he would turn to Molly and explain the intricacies of the game, and she was eager to absorb it all—as were the other fans sitting around him. He had been to a Yankee fantasy camp hosted by stars of the 1950s teams. During the camp, an unpleasant scene involving Mickey Mantle occurred, much like ones that we have all heard about. The fan's voice grew reverential when he described how Whitey Ford had tried to soothe the situation and protect his friend. He also told the story of how a rehabbing Rickey Henderson, who had been left behind after spring training, took the campers out to dinner and a prize-fight.

It seemed as though this one fan had shared countless intimate moments with great athletes, each of which had deepened his love for the game. Not only did he speak of the personal connections he had made with these players, but also he captured the sense of the brotherhood that exists among players on a team—as well as his brief membership into that club. His history was interwoven with threads of baseball lore. The screaming sixth graders didn't seem to be following the game, but Molly followed both it and her grandfather's warm stories. I was more than a little jealous of her opportunity to learn about baseball this way, at her grandfather's knee. She also played Little League, and I was sure she had been taught to throw correctly.

The SkyDome was not a very inviting place to watch an idyllic sport like base-ball, though that is understandable, as the stadium was among the first to experiment with a retractable roof. The people in the stands were generally apathetic about what was happening on the field, and their apathy was reflected back by the players. Not many players bothered to toss game balls into the stands or even seemed to acknowledge the crowd surrounding the diamond. For the fans who were enthusiastic, it was their love of the game that kept bringing them back. After extremely low attendance in the beginning of 2003 season due to a World Health Organization alert about SARS, Toronto took over first place in their division. Though they would lose this lead to the Yankees and the Red Sox, perhaps their brief dalliances with the division lead will be enough to lure fans back to SkyDome once again.

Comerica Park
Philadelphia Phillies @ Detroit Tigers
June 8, 2002
Section 124, Row 18, Seat 8

The next stop was Detroit, home of the Tigers, one of the original American League franchises. In 1905, Ty Cobb joined the Tigers. He would play for them for twenty-two years, including six as player-manager. When he retired, he held the record for hits, runs scored, and single-season stolen base totals, as well as several others. The Tigers would appear in four World Series, including three with Cobb, before finally becoming World Champs in 1935 against the Cubs. In the next decade, they would make two more World Series appearances, winning again in 1945.

In 1967, civil unrest would inundate the city of Detroit, sparking riots in July. Willie Horton, a young black player, would attempt to use his position as a Major League Baseball player to help stop the violence. He made his way to the stadium in the middle of the night, and after donning his Tigers uniform he appeared in the streets to try to quiet the masses. His role placed the Tigers organization in the forefront of the crisis, and many I spoke to in 2002 believe that when the Tigers made a successful run at a championship in 1968, the team became a means for many black and white fans to find common ground. The pride the city felt in the success of the 1968 Tigers quelled the tensions of the earlier year.

The late 1970s featured the first of an American League-record 1,918 appearances by Tiger middle infielders Alan Trammell and Lou Whitaker. In 1979, Sparky Anderson, after nine successful seasons managing the Reds, took the reins of the Tigers. He would manage the team for the next sixteen years, leading them to two division titles and a World Championship, in 1984. The Tigers have not had a winning season since 1993, and they came close to setting the record for single-season losses in 2003. The year 2004 saw the beginnings of a Tiger revival. Now, having been given a vocal commitment by ownership and a legitimate rebuilding season in 2004, fans may slowly reinvest their energy into the Tigers.

In 1999, the eighty-seven-year-old home of the Detroit Tigers, Tiger Stadium, hosted its final game. In 2000, Comerica Park opened to a sellout crowd. Tiger Stadium had been a big part of baseball history, and even though it was in need of some serious sprucing up, fans still speak of it reverentially. Comerica does not instill such loyalty. Following the riots, the city of Detroit became a symbol of urban decline. Tiger Stadium was located in one of the worst parts of the city, while Comerica is closer to the center of town. Although it is surrounded by dilapidated buildings, Comerica appears a bit like the Roman Coliseum, with large statues of tigers surrounding each entrance. I felt like I was entering a Vegas casino rather than a baseball stadium. Inside the park is a carousel, complete with tigers rather than horses to ride on, and a Ferris wheel with carriages shaped like baseballs. When I stepped inside the seating area, I could see the burned-out buildings with their missing windows that surrounded the park. The stadium seemed out of touch with the community that it was trying to support, a little like Caesars Palace might seem in downtown Beirut. Though the tiger theme around the park was fun, it seemed gaudy considering the condition of the structures surrounding the stadium.

The stadium itself was nice, but it felt cavernous. When I stepped down to the edge of the field to watch batting practice, I felt miles away from the players. Later, in my seat, I discovered that I wasn't just far away from the field but from the vendors as well. I also found that I'd lost my breath on my way through the stands to the concession area and restrooms. I couldn't even get back to the seating area before the next inning was set to begin. Though you never lose sight of the field when moving about the concourse, you don't exactly feel as though you are "in the game" either. Many fans spoke of the fine amenities in their new stadium, and one woman mentioned that she felt safer here alone than she had in the old Tiger Stadium, but most fans long for the old park nonetheless. It seems the amenities came with a price.

Much like Camden Yards, Comerica tries hard to create the feeling of an old-time stadium, yet due to the stadium's lack of comfort this attempt seems somewhat superficial. The brick walls in right and left center fields bear the names of former Tiger greats. On the left-field wall, below the line of statues, you'll see a list of players whose numbers have been retired. The right-field wall bears the names of players who have been inducted into the Baseball Hall of Fame but whose numbers have not been retired by the club. This backdrop serves as an ever-present reminder of the club's illustrious past.

When I walked around the field, I realized how far away the center fielder was from the plate. The Tigers remedied this by moving the center field fence in for the 2003 season. Without that, and without an Andruw Jones or Tori Hunter roaming the outfield, the Tigers would have had little hope for success.

There are some other very quaint aspects to the Tigers experience. Behind home plate, the singing hot dog vendor roams. His operatic voice can be heard in the far reaches of the park as he belts out the call of "Hooooooooooooot dooooooooooogs!" He also chastises all who ask for ketchup with, "What, are you from Brooklyn?" offering instead only the local favorite, mustard. During the 2004 season, the club told him that he needed to curb his repartee, as well as his bombastic singing, because fans didn't appreciate it. When fans complained about the absence of his performance, his aria was taped, and it is now played on the scoreboard. Now, the immediacy of the experience is gone. The officials at Comerica might want to rethink this decision for the future, for while his antics may have annoyed some; there is little doubt that they left a distinct and memorable impression.

Fans at Comerica are given chances to win prizes throughout the game, mostly small things, such as hot dogs and gift certificates to Baskin Robbins. The Tigers also designate each Saturday "Autograph Day," with four members of "the Tiger family" appearing for twenty minutes each to sign memorabilia for fans in two areas of the stadium. Every Friday night, the Tigers have a fireworks display in center field. During the game I attended, I noticed that a number of patrons did not arrive until the eighth inning. This allowed them to catch the pyrotechnics above the field while sparing themselves from having to watch the dismal performance of their Tigers on the field.

My overall impression was that the "Tigers family" was trying to make this new stadium feel homey and comfortable. However, until they improve the product on the field, this might be an uphill battle. Several losing seasons have made it difficult for Tigers fans to justify spending their money at the stadium. Many seemed to echo the feelings of one gentleman I spoke to, who said, "There is money for this stadium, and there is money for the Red Wings [the hockey team also owned by the Tigers' owners, the Ilitch family], but it doesn't seem that there is money to spend on baseball." In 2004, the Tigers began spending money on players again, with the most notable signing being that of Ivan Rodriguez to a multi-year deal.

The games I attended took place while the Red Wings were competing in the Stanley Cup finals in North Carolina. I was surprised at the number of fans in the stands who had their radios tuned to the hockey game. While there was not much to cheer for on the field, you would hear periodic roars as the good news came over the radio waves that the Red Wings had scored.

Detroit is clearly devoted to hockey—in fact, they pride themselves on their nickname, "Hockytown"—but the fans I talked with suggested that baseball could be loved just as much. The Tigers should be an easy sell in Detroit considering their long history, and if the new commitment from ownership is earnest, the fan base should grow quickly. If the fans don't return, though, I fear a repeat of the situation in Montreal, where the fans were blamed for the team's problems.

Michigan is a great sports state, yet the Tigers don't do enough to promote themselves and secure their share of the sports market. The stadium feels more like an amusement park than an homage to baseball, and it is so huge it would only seem natural that the Tigers would do all that they can to fill it. The Tigers need to follow the lead of the Marlins and close the upper level for most games, bringing the fans closer together.

When a team builds a new stadium, often management does its best to fill it with as many fans as possible by ensuring they have top-notch talent on the field. When Comerica opened, the Tigers tried to do just that by signing Juan Gonzalez. When that failed, their ship seemed rudderless. Now they face a new test: rebuilding. Since they were not successful at bringing in a fan favorite to build a team around, they brought in an old one, hiring Alan Trammel as field manager. Attempting to ease the suffering of Tigers fans, who were witnessing their team's worst season ever, by bringing in the former Detroit star was a bit like playing polka to lighten the mood at a funeral. However, Trammel stated that he now knew what holes management needed to fill for the 2004 squad, and that only through experimentation could the rebuilding process begin. That process is definitely in full swing, as the team won twenty-nine more games in 2004 then they had in 2003. However, while New York fans firmly believe they will likely win on any particular day, Detroit fans still have no choice but to believe that they will lose. It will take a lot more than nostalgic overtures and decent stadium amenities to make up for that.

Jacobs Field
New York Mets @ Cleveland Indians
June 9, 2002
Section 160, Row P, Seat 5

Following the second game at Comerica, I headed to Cleveland to see an inter-league game between the Indians and the Mets. Jacobs Field, or "The Jake," has a similar look to that of Comerica, but it feels much more inviting. Having gone to a few Indians games in the 1970s at Cleveland Municipal Stadium, I appreciated the openness and warmth that Jacob's Field offered. As Tom Malady said, "They do a great job of making you feel welcome." The seats are close to the field, and the crowd is enthusiastic. There was a large crowd present for batting practice, and everyone with whom I spoke glowed with pride over the stadium. They were also proud of what their team had managed to do over the past decade, signing talent and achieving success as the team moved to the new stadium. Several fans reminded me of the team's record for consecutive sellouts, although all were saddened that this would likely come to an end, since management had decided it was time to sell off their stars and rebuild the team.

The selection of food was huge considering the stadium's Midwestern location. I could feel the struggle between the club's desire to embrace its Midwestern roots (the best stadium mustard around) and its eagerness to show off the city's cosmopolitan side (by serving sushi at one food stand). Overall, the concession stands were well thought out.

Cleveland has also done a really good job of creating a couple of stars to market. With the departure of Jim Thome, Cleveland must now focus it merchandise sales on Omar Vizquel, one of the American League's first amazing shortstops. While Omar is the bridge from the old to the new, there are many talented young players to lead the team into the next decade. Vizquel, too, was lost to free agency following the 2004 season.

In early June, fans were just beginning to show disappointment with the Indians' play—and some still believed that the team would rebound. Inter-league play had created a buzz, and the fans jumped at the opportunity to see the Mets in Cleveland. In two-team cities, all the teams in the country come to play at least once, so the idea of inter-league play is not as thrilling. But in cities with one team, the chance to see the other league's players can have great appeal.

There were quite a few New Yorkers who made the trip to see the Amazins play in Cleveland, but Cleveland fans were also excited by the chance to see the "other" New York team take the field. People were hopeful that the Tribe would fare better against the Mets than they had against the Yankees. Civic pride seemed to be at stake. While driving to Cleveland, I listened to the Saturday-night game on the radio and could clearly hear New York fans cheering loudly in the stands. Following the game, the post-game show's host complained that Indians fans had allowed Mets fans to shout them down in their own stadium. The game had gone into extra innings and the Mets had won, but the announcer was clearly more upset by the Cleveland fans' apathy than the team's failure to win.

Midwesterners can be very vocal during the game, but this seems to be restricted to cheering for the good guys. When their team is winning, they vocalize their approval and admiration. When the team isn't playing well, they become a bit reserved. Fans of Eastern-seaboard teams generally feel that they always need to be heard. To them, the game is an extension of life, and they feel they need to contribute, even if this means raining boos and invectives down on their own players. Cleveland fans aren't as vocal about their feelings; rather, they show their disapproval at the turnstiles.

During 2002, season ticket holders had purchased most of the seats at Jacob's Field. Yet for the first time since the new stadium had been built, seats remained empty. When General Manger Mark Shapiro traded Bartolo Colon to the Expos for Lee Stevens and three minor leaguers, fans realized that the era of great Indians baseball was coming to an end.

Cleveland's long history in baseball began in 1869, when they fielded the precursor to the Indians, the Cleveland Spiders, whose star player from 1891 to 1899 was Cy Young. When the American League formed in 1901, the Spiders were founding members. The team was also called the Blues, then the Broncos, and in 1903 they became the Naps, in honor of star player-manager Napoleon Lajoie, who had come over from the Philadelphia Athletics. In 1910, Lajoie competed with Ty Cobb for the American League batting title. Though they were never great, the Naps fielded a strong team until 1914, when the Federal League formed, taking players from both National and American League teams. Cleveland lost a record 102 games that year, and Lajoie was replaced. With his departure the team's moniker was no longer appropriate, so the local papers announced that the new team would henceforth be known as the "Indians."

In 1920, with the addition of Tris Speaker from Boston, the Indians lead the league in many offensive categories. That year they not only won the pennant but also beat the Brooklyn Dodgers in the best-of-nine World Series. Though the 1920s saw a few second-place finishes, it would be quite awhile before the Tribe would win another pennant. Their second-place finish in 1940 included a twenty-seven-win season by right-handed pitcher Bob Feller. Before enlisting in the military in 1941, Feller would accumulate 107 wins over his first seven big-league seasons. Also in 1941, Lou Boudreau became player-manager, and in 1944 he won the American League batting title.

In 1946, the Indians got a new owner, Bill Veeck. Between his promotional skills and his ability to sign great baseball talent (including the American League's first African-American, Lary Doby), Veeck would both double attendance and lead the Indians back to a World Series within one year. (They advanced to the Series after a one-game playoff with the Red Sox in 1948.) Bill Veeck left the Indians after the 1949 season and bought the St. Louis Browns, but the Indians remained competitive throughout the next decade. From 1951 until 1956, the Indians finished second behind the Yankees in every year but one. That year,

1954, they won the pennant but were swept in the World Series by another New York team, the Giants.

During the 1960s and 1970s, the Indians suffered great economic hardship, with ownership changing seven times in twenty-five years. The 1968 team was the only team between 1960 and 1993 to finish as high as third place.

In 1986 two prominent local businessmen were financing a mall in downtown Cleveland, and they felt they needed the Indians to anchor the project. The Jacobs brothers purchased the team, and the rebuilding—of both the roster and a new stadium—began. A levy on tobacco and alcohol was passed in 1990 to finance the new field, and new management was brought in to grow a strong farm system. The new stadium opened in 1994, and by 1995, with attendance consistently high, a team capable of winning the American League pennant was fielded. Although the Indians eventually lost to the Atlanta Braves in the World Series in six games, Jacobs Field sold out the entire 1996 season before opening day. The Indians lost to Baltimore in the divisional series that year, but they would return to the World Series in 1997, losing to the expansion Florida Marlins. In 1998, the division-winning Indians would lose to the 125-game-winning Yankees in the ALCS. In 1999, Cleveland won its fifth straight and most recent division title. Both 2000 and 2001 were exciting but disappointing seasons for Indians fans, and the team's slow start in 2002 made it apparent that the run was over. The team kept a low profile in 2003, but they finished a little stronger than expected in the weak AL Central Division.

Standing in line outside the stadium, I met parents of a young fan who had never known the Tribe as a losing franchise. The Indians should take great care not to lose the momentum they have built over the past decade, which has seen the Indians go from perennial basement dweller to the community's crowning jewel. The 2004 season, with big bats returning to the Indians lineup, proved that this shouldn't be a problem.

Qualcomm Stadium
New York Yankees @ San Diego Padres
June 22, 2002
Section Plaza 16, Row 10, Seat 1

At the end of June, I headed for the longest leg of the journey, California, where I would see twelve games in twelve days. When I finished this tour, just prior to the All-Star break, I would be exactly halfway through the majors. I started in the South, with the Padres.

After years of hosting the minor-league Padres, San Diego was granted a major-league franchise in 1968. They began play in 1969. In 1977, Padres pitchers Rollie Fingers and Bob Owchinko earned the NL Fireman of the Year and Rookie Pitcher of the Year awards respectively, and the following year Gaylord Perry won the National League Cy Young Award. In 1980, Fingers would earn his third consecutive Fireman of the Year award, while the Padres would become the first major-league club to have three players, Gene Richards, Ozzie Smith, and Jerry Mumphrey, with fifty stolen bases each.

In 1984, fifteen years after they began play, the Padres played in their first World Series, against the Detroit Tigers. They lost the series, but Tony Gwynn won the first of eight National League batting titles that season. San Diego got to the World Series again in 1998, but they were swept by the New York Yankees.

Dave Winfield, who played with the Padres from 1973 to 1980, became the first player to enter the Baseball Hall of Fame in Cooperstown wearing a Padres cap, when he was inducted in 2001. The Padres have had many exceptional players over the years, but they have fielded few noteworthy teams.

In 1973, after only four years in the major leagues, the Padres were put up for sale. When financing for a deal that would have moved the team to Washington, D.C., fell through, Ray Kroc, founder of the McDonalds food chain and a baseball fan, swooped in and bought the team, ensuring that they would remain in San Diego. When Kroc passed away in 1984, just months before the Padres' first World Series appearance, ownership passed to his wife, Joan. In 1987, Joan Kroc decided that she didn't want to be involved with baseball anymore. She tried to sell the franchise to the city of San Diego to ensure that the Padres would not be moved to another town. The other MLB owners, fearing that municipal ownership would grant a government entity too much power in the operations of baseball and give politicians a controlling voice in the business, vetoed the sale.[11]

Through 2003, the Padres played at Qualcomm Stadium (originally Jack Murphy Stadium, named after the original owner), also the home of the San Diego Chargers. This series was the only time I would see the Yankees play on the road, which was an interesting experience in itself. How many Yankee fans could there be in San Diego? A lot. I was amazed at the number of Yankee fans present in San Diego, surely a result of the team's recent successes. The parking lot is enormous and features quite possibly the largest tailgate contingent in Major League Baseball. (I said *possibly*, Brewers fans.) As I wandered around the parking lot I saw a lot of military personnel, which is natural considering that three military bases are located nearby. Many were huge Yankees fans, while others positively despised them. As is true elsewhere, the Yankees had polarized the fans in attendance that day. I didn't find anyone who was as passionate about the Padres until I was inside—with the exception of two drunk guys who bragged of proudly giving Derek Jeter the finger as he rode in on the team bus. I didn't have the heart to tell them that the shortstop had been at the stadium two hours prior to this media bus's arrival.

Qualcomm is surrounded by a wall that separates it from the mammoth parking lot outside. Once inside the wall, I found countless vendors of food and merchandise, as well as ramps, elevators, and escalators to allow you to move to your seats. One area unique to San Diego is the trading pin booth, where fans can purchase a pin and hang it on the wall and then take a pin left by a fan of another team. Merchandise booths here are filled with souvenirs from each major league franchise. Inside the pin booth, I overheard one woman remark, "That woman said that you can't get other teams' merchandise at the team store in New York." Though most stadiums will put out a couple of items for the visiting team, Padres' store made sure all teams were well represented. This was a second clear signal to me that the Padres were not surviving on their name alone.

Inside the seating area, I found a couple of season ticket holders down the right-field line. One explained that most of the ticket holders whom she knew "wouldn't come to such an over-hyped game." This made sense at the time, but I do think that any serious aficionado of the sport would want to see the Yankees play at least once. At any rate, most of the people there that day were not everyday Padres fans, a fact that led me to think that there might not be many true fans of the team at all. I got the impression that the main reason the Padres exist is to showcase other MLB teams to the large deposit of military personnel located in the area.

Surprisingly, the games were very close, with Ted Lilly pitching a gem for the Yankees against Jake Peavey in his ML debut. The Yankees won by a 1-0 score, with Alfonso Soriano scoring in the first inning. The two pitchers gave up only three hits each. Both games were great, and I had a wonderful vantage from my seat down the left-field line.

That season, the Padres encouraged fan involvement through a number of fun activities, including a "guess-the-attendance" game, in which a fan rearranges numbered placards while the crowd cheers him or her on and screams suggestions, sort of like something you might see on *The Price is Right*.

The stadium was clearly more suited to football (though the Chargers ownership seems unhappy with the current situation in San Diego), so the Padres opened their own stadium in the downtown area in 2004. Though many fans I spoke with seemed upset that their famous tailgate parties would come to an end, they were hopeful about the chance to see the game in more intimate surroundings. As in Cleveland, the San Diego management was mindful of the need to put a competitive club on the field when they moved into their new stadium. With a crop of good young players, and a few experienced veterans, they made a good run at the wild card in 2004 before injuries took their toll.

It was during this 2002 Saturday game that the passing of Darryl Kile was announced. Since I was on the West Coast, I didn't hear about it until after that first afternoon game in San Diego. The Cubs-Cardinals game that day had been canceled, and the two teams were scheduled to play the next night, on ESPN Sunday Night Baseball. Following the Sunday afternoon game in San Diego, I headed up the freeway and listened to the game on the radio. For West Coast fans, catching this broadcast is easy, since it begins at 5:00 P.M. local time and is usually over by 9:00 P.M., whereas in the East the game can drag on until midnight, which places a strain on listeners who have to get up early for work the next day. I couldn't imagine anything finer than driving along the coast while listening to the game, yet it broke my heart to listen to the announcers calling the game while the fans remained silent in the background, clearly in mourning. When Albert Pujols hit a meaningless two-run home run, you couldn't help but hope that something divine was happening and that the Cardinals would pull ahead for the win. That didn't happen. I was glad for the quiet crowd at Wrigley when the game came to end.

Dodger Stadium
Colorado Rockies @ Los Angeles Dodgers
June 24, 2004,
Loge 151, Row E, Seat 4

I arrived at my hotel at the conclusion of the Cardinals-Cubs game. The final score was 8-3, Cubs. Over the next few days I would see the Dodgers play the Rockies. I had met a few Rockies coaches earlier in the season, but since they lived in the Los Angeles area, I assumed that I wouldn't see any at the hotel during this trip. Other members of the Colorado team were everywhere, though, including an injured Benny Agbayani, who spent hours walking his one-year-old daughter around the lobby.

I had never been to Dodger Stadium, so I was excited to see it, especially since it was one of the few old parks remaining. The Dodgers had been a New York team until 1958, and quite a successful one. When New York Director of Parks Robert Moses put up roadblocks to Walter O'Malley's plan to build a ballpark for his team in a more central location, the Dodgers owner began exploring other options. As fortune would have it, the mayor of Los Angeles came to New York that year in hopes of finding a team willing to move to his city. With the population shift that had occurred following World War II, as well as the growing success the Yankees were having in the New York market, O'Malley jumped at the chance to move the team to the West Coast and tap into the new California market. Along with the New York Giants, the team headed to the Pacific, supplanting the St. Louis Cardinals as the westernmost Major League Baseball franchise.

For the first four years, they played at the Los Angeles Coliseum, a stadium not conducive to baseball; then, in 1962, they moved to their present-day home, Dodger Stadium. With the fantastic pitching duo of Sandy Koufax and Don Drysdale, the Dodgers looked like they might be as successful on the field in L.A. as they had been in Brooklyn. They won the National League pennant in 1963, 1965, and 1966, and the World Series in both 1963 and 1965. In the 1970s, no Dodger team ever finished lower than third. They also fielded the same starting infield—first baseman Steve Garvey, second baseman Davey Lopes, shortstop Bill Russell, and third baseman Ron Cey—from 1973 until 1981, a record that still stands. Tommy Lasorda began managing the team in 1977 and led them to consecutive pennants in 1977 and 1978, and then again in 1981, winning the World Series in the final two years. Again, these years were marked by consistency in the field, but also by great pitchers, including Fernando Valenzuela, a cult hero among Mexicans and Mexican-Americans, and Orel Hershiser, who in 1988 set the major-league record for consecutive scoreless innings pitched, with fifty-nine. Hershiser also helped his team to reach the World Series that year, where they beat the favored Oakland Athletics.

The 1990s for the Dodgers were marked by successes on the field and at the draft table. They became the only team in history to have a player win Rookie of the Year honors for five straight years.

The Dodgers haven't won a pennant since 1988, despite sitting among the top five teams in baseball in spending since 1995. Fox bought the Dodgers in 1999 for $311 million and sold them to Boston businessman Frank McCourt for $430 million in 2004, when they won their division.

I remember the Dodgers of the late 1960s and 1970s. They had been the Reds' biggest rivals in the National League West. Somehow they always seemed to receive a lot of press coverage, and I still have Technicolor images of Don Drysdale etched in my mind. What I didn't realize until I entered Dodger Stadium was that these images of a tanned Drysdale, with palm trees in the background, had not been recorded during spring training. These images had been shot here, at Dodger Stadium.

My eyes welled up with tears as I entered, and I felt the same reverence for this place that I feel for Yankee Stadium. The sun, shining in a beautiful blue sky, illuminated the colors of the stadium, bringing back memories of the Technicolor images I had seen on television when I was a girl. It felt like a stadium, but with the foothills in the background, it also felt so much more open and rural than I had expected it to be, given its urban locale. It seemed like a great place to watch baseball, and I was very excited to be there.

Unfortunately, my overall experience was not as wonderful as my first impression. I wanted to move to all corners of the stadium and to talk to fans everywhere. Unfortunately, I quickly found that without a press pass I couldn't move to any level other than the one my ticket granted me access to, not even during batting practice. I had already missed the home team's batting practice so I needed to move around quickly to talk to as many fans as possible on my level. I had often heard that Dodger fans come late and leave early, and this did seem to be true. Traffic in Los Angeles during the two hours prior to game time is horrendous, largely explaining why so many people straggle in throughout the first three or four innings.

The parking lot, which is owned by the city of Los Angeles, charges a fee that's more expensive than a ticket to the bleachers. Yet given the state of public transportation in the area, and the remoteness of the stadium, it is almost impossible to arrive by means other than car. Though the tickets seemed reasonably priced given that the Dodgers play in baseball's second largest media market, the additional cost of parking puts a day at the stadium out of reach for most.

The early crowd consisted mostly of young twenty-somethings. Many were students who didn't have full-time work. I also met a few older folks who had come to games at the Coliseum with their dads; they were happy to provide me with stories to go along with the images in my memory.

The Dodgers were doing well in the standings while I was there, despite the recent visit of the Red Sox for inter-league play. Along with the Giants, they were in the hunt for the National League West lead, trying to catch the Diamondbacks. The Rockies played well during my first game, and the Dodgers made a lot of mistakes, including an error by Cesar Izturis to put the first base runner of the game on board. The Rockies won 4-1.

The next night, the Dodgers played a much better game. Although the Rockies' John Thomson gave up only five hits (including two home runs) throughout eight innings, he was outmatched by Dodgers' Odalis Perez, who only allowed two base runners the whole night—one on a two-out walk in the second and the other on the only Colorado hit, by Bobby Estalella, in the sixth. The game was over in less than two hours.

Despite the beauty of the stadium, it felt dated. The concourse is dark, and the concessions are located in small, poorly situated areas, which seemed to be at odds with the sprawling feel of California.

The Dodgers have a large season-ticket base, and most of the seats are sold out long before game day. While this sounds great in theory, the Dodgers would benefit greatly from a program where ticket holders could resell unused tickets. In theater, tickets that can't be used on a particular date can often be exchanged for tickets to later performances. If the club allowed people to resell their tickets in this manner, they might have a better chance of filling the stands. Creating a sense of a full stadium might increase the team's popularity and make attracting advertisers easier.

In 2003, the team once again had a disappointing season, but I'm sure their race for the division in 2004, and their advancement to the first round of the play-offs, made the difficult drive to the stadium worthwhile. Moves following the season also will make the Dodgers and interesting team to watch, as they attempt to better their 2004 success.

Pac Bell Park
San Diego Padres @ San Francisco Giants
June 26, 2002,
Section 127, Row 2, Seat 6

I arrived at Pac Bell at noon for a 1:35 P.M. game. As I approached, I saw swarms of people everywhere. I had heard how enormously popular Pacific Bell Park was, but I couldn't have imagined that there would be this many people there this early. It seemed as though the stadium would be full more than an hour before game time, which rarely happens anywhere. I would soon realize that the starting time for this game had been changed almost two months earlier. The Giants' opponents, the Padres, had a schedule conflict with the Chargers for use of their stadium in early September. The Giants agreed to switch the location of two games of this four game series with two games of the September set to alleviate the problem. I was here for the third game, the first one back at Pac Bell. Because the teams now had to travel between cities, this game had been moved to an hour later. Most ticket holders had not heard about the schedule change, despite the teams numerous attempts to publicize it. As a result, the fans were filling the park very early in the day. The stadium was nearly sold out for a mid-week day game.

Harry Stoneham, the owner of the NY Giants in 1957, was losing the war at the turnstiles for New York fans. When O'Malley of the Dodgers approached him about moving West, he jumped at the chance. The Giants needed a new park with additional parking in order to remain competitive. By moving to California, Stoneham would gain large territorial rights and get his new stadium at the same time. As the story goes, however, the San Francisco mayor wanted the Giants to relocate West but didn't want to give up prime real estate for a new park. He took Stoneham to Candlestick Point at a time of day when the winds were at their calmest, and he was able to sell him on the site. Stoneham thought it was a marvelous location, and Candlestick Park was built. It wasn't until the team had been there for a while that they realized how cold and windy the setting was going to be.

Forty years later, in 2000, the Giants opened Pacific Bell Park. In 2003, SBC Communications bought Pacific Bell and the name of the park was changed to SBC Park. It is the only privately funded baseball park in the major leagues today; less than 7% of its costs came from public sources. Funds for the park were raised through corporations and individuals, and lifetime charters were sold for each seat.

In order to purchase a season ticket, you must first purchase the lifetime rights to your seat. The most expensive of these rights sold for $7,500, while seats in the upper deck went for $1,500. This fee is paid before the tickets themselves are purchased, and they are on the high end of major-league ticket prices. Of course, this meant that many of the loyal fans who suffered through the winds of Candlestick could not afford even the worst seats at the new Pac Bell Park. True baseball fans need to be aware of this before they vote against new stadium levies. Teams can often fund stadiums themselves, but in so doing they might make it difficult for the everyday fan to afford seats. The downside for the Giants is that once the novelty of Pac Bell/SBC wears off in San Francisco, they will have 45,000 empty seats, no matter how good the team is (and Barry Bonds isn't going to play forever).

I attended a mid-week day game filled with folks playing hooky from work. It was the day after the fight in the dugout between Bonds and Jeff Kent had been caught by live television cameras. Listening to the radio before the game, I discovered a new perspective on the whole Kent vs. Bonds situation. In the East, all one ever hears is how self-centered Bonds can be, with his lounge chair, his four lockers, and all his other luxuries. But once in San Francisco, I discovered that Kent is no prince either. I had missed his time in New York, where I later found out no one liked him either. Bonds may be bad, but Kent seems egotistical and intolerant. Today is another day full of new perspectives, I thought.

Pac Bell/SBC is a beautiful park, much how I remember Camden Yards when it first opened. The food smelled fantastic, and the choices were varied. It was so crowded that it was a little hard to move around—and this is definitely a park that's worth walking all the way around. The view from the right-field brick wall is amazing, both looking in and looking out. Underneath, one can watch a few innings of the game for free, as a nod to the old knothole gangs. Not a bad way to pass a lunch hour.

In left field, there is a giant Coke bottle slide and an oversized glove, symbols of corporate sponsorship that represent someone's idea of what "family entertainment" at a ballgame should be. How can you make fans of the game if the kids spend all their time on the slide and mom and dad are running back and forth trying to keep an eye on them?

While in left field, I spotted two ladies sitting at the back of the bleachers wearing sunhats covered in Giants pins and wearing sweatshirts and scarves bearing the team logo. They stood out among the conservatively dressed crowd, so I decided to introduce myself. A mother and daughter, they attended games regularly with another daughter and her husband, who were also there that day. Though the couple was not as elaborately adorned in team gear, the four were among the most loyal baseball fans I had met in California. The mother had grown up playing baseball with her brothers as a young girl in California and later attended San Francisco Seals games. She loved her Seals, and when the Giants came to San Francisco, she immediately embraced the major-league team. These women had been season ticket holders at Candlestick for years, but when the new park opened, they couldn't afford seats. Eventually, they discovered that a number of affordable handicap and senior citizen season seats were available in the outfield. They signed up, and now they get to many games each year. Though they missed the atmosphere of Candlestick, they did not miss the temperature. Most of the older fans they had met at Candlestick could not come to games anymore—or at least not as regularly—due to the high-ticket prices.

The ladies insisted that I watch the game from the upper deck so I could be near the few "real fans" who had come over from the old park. The mother glowed as she recounted great stories about seeing Orlando Cepeda and a young

Willie Mays play. Every year, the family also went to a few A's games, which were more affordable, but Giants were always their first choice. Later, when I met other people from the area and mentioned these ladies, I gained instant credibility for having met the real fans. I was comforted to find them sitting in their left-field seats during the third game of the 2002 World Series when Fox picked them out during one of its pan shots of the crowd.

The game itself turned out to be an exciting match up, though Bonds was not scheduled to play that day. It was a day game following a very late night game in San Diego, and Bonds would get the day off. At the end of the second inning, the score was tied 1-1, with the Padres doing a great job of getting on base but blowing their opportunities. In the fourth, the Giants took advantage of Padres pitcher Oliver Perez. First, Benito Santiago earned a walk, and then he moved to second after J. T. Snow was hit by a pitch. Third baseman Pedro Feliz then hit a single to right, and Santiago scored. Shinjo sacrificed the runners over another base, but the Giants pitcher, Kirk Reuter, struck out looking for the final out. The Padres would not let the run go unanswered, and Reuter had a rough go upon returning to the mound. The Padres ended up scoring four runs off of four hits and a walk before Reuter could get catcher Tom Lampkin to hit a ground ball for the third out. Reuter returned in the sixth to retire the side in order.

The score remained 5-2 Padres until the bottom of the ninth. Santiago singled to left, and Snow moved him over with a second hit to left field. With two men on and the tying run coming to the plate, Bonds was announced as the pinch hitter. Of course, Bonds was walked, leaving Marvin Bernard to do the work. He hit a long fly ball to center field. From first, Bonds could see that it wouldn't be caught, but Snow had no such view on second. Bonds took off and quickly caught up to Snow, who had hesitated in case he needed to tag up. Realizing that Bonds knew what was happening, Snow took off. Santiago crossed the plate and then turned to signal to the runners. I was sitting behind the third base dugout, and with Bonds tight on Snow's heels, I could hear him yelling "Go go go go," as Snow worked hard to stay in front of the still very quick slugger. Santiago signaled for Bonds to slide, but Snow, thinking the signal was for him, dropped down, scoring the second run. Unfortunately, his slide made it difficult for Bonds to touch the plate, and he became the victim of a great throw to the Padres catcher. Bernard had managed to get to third and would score two batters later.

The game was tied, and everyone who had been disappointed that Bonds wasn't in the starting lineup had been treated to a fantastic surprise. Though people often say Bonds is getting old, for a few minutes I couldn't imagine anyone faster. Even at his age, he'd had to slow down so as not to pass the base runner ahead of him.

Rob Nen came in the tenth and retired his three batters in order, and in the bottom of the tenth, Reggie Sanders and Kent both grounded out, bringing Santiago to the plate. He singled to left, and then Snow doubled to right. Bonds was intentionally walked to load the bases, and Bernard came up again. Unfortunately, he grounded to short for the third out, stranding the runners. The score remained tied until the bottom of the twelfth.

With Rodney Myers on the mound for the Padres, Sanders led off the inning with a walk, followed quickly by base on balls to Kent. Santiago laid down a textbook bunt to move the runners over, and J. T. Snow hit a shot up the middle to single in the winning run. In a game that seemed to belong to the Padres through eight innings, the Giants had come out on top. I didn't know it at the time, but this game would prove to be a microcosm of the Giants entire season.

For the second game, also a mid-week day game, I sat upstairs. The view upon entering the upper deck was spectacular. There is nothing like it anywhere, and on a sunny day in San Francisco, I wouldn't want to be anywhere else. I realized the downside of sitting in the upper deck about an hour into the game. Since it is pretty steep, you get a spectacular view of the bay, and your eye naturally drifts to the boats coming in and out of the harbor. Some of the seats don't give you a vantage of the area behind home base either, so it's hard to remain focused on the game, even an exciting one. This area would be a great place to bring non-baseball fans visiting from out of town. Baseball fans, however, might find it unrewarding. The advantage to sitting upstairs, though, is the joy of being surrounded by people who really, really love the game—people who live and die with their Giants.

Downstairs, the day before, fans had spent the afternoon discussing business and talking on their cell phones. No one was really vocal in his or her appreciation of the Giants. One gentleman who seemed to like baseball told me how he had to buy the charter seats because his wife had served on the committee to raise money for Pac Bell. This was a typical scenario for those sitting downstairs. He wasn't willing to pay for the seats behind home, but the ones out by third were fine. Few people in this area had attended many games at Candlestick. Upstairs, the fans were different. Everyone shared their opinions about the action on the field with each other, loudly, seemingly in the hope that Dusty Baker might actually hear them. They made friends with their neighbors as they commiserated about batting and pitching changes. These guys knew every stat and every player. When a couple among them cheered for the Padres, the home rooters teased them mercilessly—until they recognized the couple as equally loyal and knowl-edgeable Padres fans. For a brief three hours, I felt for the first time during my trip to California that people for whom the world rested on the outcome of the game surrounded me. Their passion seeped into me, and I remained on the edge of my chair all day.

This game, much like the first, was an unexpected treat. It was during the pre-vious night that Dusty Baker awoke with the idea to bat Jeff Kent in front of Barry Bonds. The second baseman would get more pitches to hit, and with his talent he would do more with them than the others who had been there. Baker was proven right. Kent went three for five that day, with two doubles. Rookie Ryan Jensen was pitching for the Giants, and he quickly got into trouble, giving up hits and watching his infielders fumble grounders. The Padres scored five runs and batted through the side before Jensen could produce the third out. Kevin Jarvis started strong for the Padres, allowing only one base runner until the third. Then San Francisco returned the favor from the first, also scoring five runs while forcing a couple of errors out of San Diego. Jarvis was removed from the mound before the inning was over.

The score remained tied until the bottom of the sixth, when the Giants whit-tled away at the new pitcher until they loaded the bases. With two outs, Kent came up to bat. He hit a double to knock in three runs. Bonds was intentionally walked, and Reggie Sanders hit a grounder to short for the third out. In the eighth, the Padres sent up Gene Kingsale to pinch-hit, and he hit a meaningless home run. (It was meaningless to the score, but not to him—it was his first homer in the big leagues despite having spent part of every season since 1996 with a major-league club.) The fans around me began to get nervous, but Aaron Fultz, the Giants pitcher, struck out the next guy easily. He was then replaced with Tim Worrell so the Giants could get the lefty-righty match-up. Worrell walked one man but then managed to get the Padres second baseman, Ramon Vasquez, to ground into a double play, ending the inning. The Giants added three more runs, putting the game out of sight. Worrell stayed in the game, but after he loaded the bases by giving up two hits and a walk, Rob Nen was brought in to close for the Giants in the top of the ninth. He struck out Ron Gant, and then Deivi Cruz hit a ball into short right center. Bonds and Rich Aurilia both charged the ball, but neither was close. Both seemed a bit timid, as though they feared an injury-causing collision. Tsuyoshi Shinjo was also charging from center; upon realizing the ball was going to fall between the two closer to it, he dove. Not only did he catch the ball at the last second before it hit the ground, but he also came up ready to throw home. No one dared leave their bag. Nen struck out the last batter, and the game was over.

These Giants games are among the most memorable that I saw that season. Pac Bell was the middle stop on my California tour, and it was here that I began to see what California baseball fans were really like. It's hard sometimes to tell much about a group of baseball fans until you watch games like these. I couldn't help but get swept up in the excitement—rooting for the home team was easy here given the loud, heartfelt cheering in the upper deck.

The next day the Giants began an inter-league series against the A's across town. Though I had just seen the Padres play before coming here, switching allegiances hadn't been that hard. The Padres home games hadn't inspired me, since I was mostly surrounded by Yankees fans. Switching allegiances tomorrow was going to be tough.

Oakland Coliseum
San Francisco Giants @ Oakland Athletics
June 28, 2002,
Section 223, Row 5, Seat 11

Seeing the A's would be a unique experience for me, since I wasn't going to see their games back to back. The first would be a Friday-night game against the Giants, and the second would be Monday against the Twins. I felt that both games would be great, but for different reasons. One opponent was a cross-town rival and the other was the young upstart team that was running away with the American League Central. In between the two games, I would need to drive back down to Anaheim to see the Angels play the Dodgers.

When I arrived at Network Associates Coliseum, I headed to the sidelines past the A's dugout and found a lot of fans watching the A's warm up. Several yelled greetings to the players, who turned and waved back. One fellow who attended a great number of games each year called out to Tim Hudson to tell him that he'd really liked the interview Hudson had given the night before. Hudson turned and hesitantly shared his fear that he had sounded too hokey. When the fan told him that he hadn't, and that he thought Hudson was right on, Hudson thanked him and ran to the bullpen to warm up. Other fans yelled to specific players, and the players not only recognized these folks but chided one or two for missing a previous game. The players here know their real fans and demonstrate a great amount of respect for them. The players also seemed to be happy to be out on the field, as opposed to the players in Toronto. If I had to guess a reason for this, I'd say it was a result of their lower-than-average team age—they have few veterans who have had time to grow aloof.

The Bay-area teams had the most ethnically diverse crowds I had seen thus far. While the Angels have a large Mexican-American population and the New York teams have a large Hispanic contingent, the A's and the Giants have many African-Americans in the stands in addition to their Caucasian and Latino supporters. The Bay-area teams themselves are also made up of players from various backgrounds, but that doesn't begin to explain why the A's are able to draw an ethnically diverse crowd while Kansas City and Chicago are not.

Network Associates' Coliseum is a large cement structure, built for baseball but with the feel of a football stadium. Many people reminded me that it had been a better venue before Al Davis forced Alameda County, the Coliseum's owners and operators, to build luxury boxes in the outfield in order to lure his Raiders back to Oakland. The idyllic nature of baseball is lost here—there are Ramada Inns with more character—but unlike the Marlins' home, which actually is a football stadium, the Coliseum does have its benefits. The stadium is pretty easy to move around in. There are a lot of food choices, and they are spread around the stadium pretty well, though I thought there were too few vendors in the stands for a Friday night against the cross-town rival.

The Philadelphia Athletics, founded in 1901, were one of the original American League teams. After little success, including twenty seasons between 1934 and 1954 where they finished fourth or lower in the standings, the team was sold and moved to Kansas City. The bad luck continued in the new city, where they finished under .500 in their first thirteen seasons.

Charley Finley bought the club in 1960. Following a failed attempt to move the team to Dallas, Finley succeeded in relocating them to Oakland in 1968. Beginning in 1969, the tide shifted for the Oakland Athletics. They won eighty-eight games that year, a total they would surpass in each of their next six seasons. The A's won three consecutive World Series from 1972 to 1974. Under different ownership, they reached the Series in three consecutive years from 1988 to 1990, winning in 1989.

Charley Finley, the man responsible for relocating the A's to Oakland, was among the first to see the benefits of packaging the game to maximize its entertainment value. He came up with the color scheme for the A's uniforms, and the mix-and-match style that went along with it. At one point, he tried to convince the league to use orange baseballs so fans could follow the ball better as it moved. He also urged the commissioner to stage World Series games at night so that fans who worked during the day could attend. Unfortunately, the idea was so success-ful that now all Series games are played at night—to both maximize the television audience and reap the most advertising dollars.

Finley was disliked by many of the other owners at the time, both for his gruff manner and for his tinkering with the game. He was looked down upon for the way he used the press as a tool to drum up publicity. In one incident, he signed a young pitcher, Jim Hunter, and nicknamed him "Catfish" after a fictitious inci-dent that created a media buzz about the young pitcher. He was also known for his feuds with players, once firing an infielder because he had made two errors in one game.

He also demonstrated the real downside of free agency. In 1976, to avoid expensive arbitration with prospective free agents while attendance was lagging, he sold three stars—Joe Rudi and Rollie Fingers to the Red Sox and Vida Blue to the Yankees—for cash and no prospects. Commissioner Bowie Kuhn voided the sale, reasoning that the shift of so much talent away from one club to two already strong teams would "be bad for the interests of baseball." Rudi, Fingers, and five other free agents played out their options and then moved to other teams the fol-lowing year. Finley was again rebuilding with young talent when he sold the team in 1981.

The A's/Giants game was a passion-filled experience for me. The fans were vocal and the game was exciting, featuring some top-notch baseball. The Giants led 3-2 through the fourth, but in the fifth, Livan Hernandez got into trouble and gave up four earned runs before being replaced by Jay Witasick. Witasick eas-ily got the last out in the fifth, but in the sixth he gave up four earned runs while struggling to get the third out. The Giants had a mini-rally in the ninth, scoring three runs, but in the end the A's prevailed 10-6.

The second game I saw, against the Twins two nights later, was a close one, with the two teams trading the lead several times until the top of the seventh, when the Twins pulled ahead 5-4. Tori Hunter even gave the crowd a preview of his All-Star Game performance by reaching over the wall and stealing what would have been John Mabry's second home run of the day.

The crowd was smaller for the Twins game, which was not surprising consid-ering the near sell-out weekend that it followed. The Twins starting pitcher, rookie Kyle Losche, was a hometown kid, and many in the stands were there to cheer him on. Despite this, the most meaningful connections that night, as on the previous night, were between the A's and their faithful fans, who seemed to call out to each other in equal measure.

Athletics fans have to feel good about their team, not only because of their success on the field (despite a limited budget) but also because of the players comfort level at reaching out to the fans. In 2001, J. P. Ricciardi left the Oakland A's front office to become general manager of the Toronto Blue Jays. It's a shame he wasn't able to bring a little of that community spirit along with him.

Edison International Field
Los Angeles Dodgers @ Anaheim Angels
June 29, 2002,
Section F 104, Row U, Seat 1

The Anaheim Angels began play in 1961 as the California Angels. It would be eighteen years before they would appear in the post season, despite many stellar performances from some of the game's most talented athletes. Their first really big star, Nolan Ryan, began shining in 1973. On May 15 of that season, his second with the Halos, he threw his first no-hitter against the Royals, and later that same season he repeated the feat against the Tigers, becoming only the fifth pitcher to throw two in the same season. Ryan would throw two more no-hitters for the Angels, his third coming on his forty-first and final start of the year in 1974. In his eight years with the Angels, he pitched fewer than 220 innings only once.

Let's put that into perspective. There were sixteen pitchers to pitch 220 innings in 2002. Of those, only eight had pitched at least five full seasons in the majors, and of those eight, only Tom Glavine, Curt Schilling, and Randy Johnson had pitched 220 innings in six or more seasons. Roger Clemens and Greg Maddux are the only other active pitchers to accomplish this feat, though neither pitched over 200 innings in 2002.

By the end of the 1970s, the Angels started making post-season appearances, led by 1979 Most Valuable Player Don Baylor and former Twins star Rod Carew. The Halos lost to Baltimore in the ALCS in 1979 and to Milwaukee in 1982. In 1984, Reggie Jackson, playing on his fourth team, hit his five hundredth career home run. Also that year, Mike Witt pitched the Angels' first perfect game. In 1986, Don Sutton won his three hundredth game, and the Angels again entered the ALCS as the Western Division champion. Unfortunately, they would lose that series in heartbreaking fashion to the Boston Red Sox. It wasn't until 2002 that the Angels, now from Anaheim, were able to break their streak of bad luck in the American League Championship Series and win the World Series, defeating the San Francisco Giants.

The Anaheim Angels played some of the best baseball I would see in 2002, including this first series against the Dodgers during the last weekend of inter-league play. I was unprepared for the sellout crowds I would encounter for the entire series. The rumor among the Angels' faithful was that this was all the fault of Dodgers fans, who commonly snatched up all their tickets. Unlike New York or Chicago, where heated cross-town rivalries exist, California fans don't feel ani-mosity for the "other" team in their cities, although the rivalries between the north and south are fierce.

When the Dodgers and Giants arrived in California in 1958, an immediate natural rivalry was born. The emergence of American League franchises did little to hinder the National League fans' loyalty to their teams, nor did it soften their enmity for their rivals. The Angels and the A's both benefited from proximity to baseball-loving fans. Both Giants and Dodgers supporters see the inter-league match-ups as an opportunity to watch great players compete in a different venue, where tickets are more plentiful and a little cheaper at that. Also, the New York and Chicago rivalries developed while both local teams were vying for champion-ships in the same season. In the California cities, both teams have rarely had suc-cessful seasons at the same time, so rooting for both local teams allows fans to bask in the glow of success more often. The Giants-Dodgers rivalry also mirrors the rivalry between the city of Los Angeles and the city of San Francisco, each of whom would like to claim that their town is the best metropolis in the state.

Though I found few people who really loved the Angels—like the Padres fans, they chose to stay away from the fanatical Dodgers fans—I did meet a lot of Angels fans as I traveled to other stadiums. It seems as though each player on the Angels' roster has his own following—from Tim Salmon and David Eckstein to Garrett Anderson and Scott Spiezio. This trend is reflected in the team store, which offers jerseys featuring the names and numbers of virtually all the players. You get the sense that although Angels fans are proud of their past stars, they are excited about their team as a whole and place no one player above the rest.

The people of Los Angeles act as if a visit to Anaheim is like going to the ends of the earth, though this is largely because of the traffic that plagues the city. However, the Angels make the trek worthwhile. The giveaways during the game include round-trip airline tickets, and the crowd participates in creating the high-light reel shown between innings by voting on the greatest play made during the previous series. And though it may seem difficult to get to the stadium for Los Angeles residents, it is difficult to find a parking lot that is easier to get out of following the game. Once I pulled out of my parking space, I never stopped again until I was at my hotel.

Aaron Sele pitched a two-hit complete game, and the Angels showed their scrappiness right away, with Eckstein hitting a hard ball that the shortstop was able to stop but not field and moving to second on a wild pitch. He finally scored on a hit-and-run single by Tim Salmon. The Angels never let up, and the final score was 7-0.

Behind me sat a couple from Great Britain that had been transferred here for work. Friends had brought them to a baseball game when they first arrived—a very American thing to do—and they had fallen in love with the game. "Much more of a team sport than cricket," said the husband, who felt cricket was too boring. They came often and had fallen in love with the Angels, not just baseball. The young man sitting next to me couldn't decide which team he liked better. He was wearing his Angels cap, but he was really rooting for Paul Lo Duca and the Dodgers. Just as I was thinking about the unbelievably white uniforms that the Angels were sporting, this young man asked me if I had noticed how the Dodgers home whites glowed under the lights at Chavez Ravine. I stared blankly at him for a minute or two while I processed the coincidence.

The next night the Angels beat the division-leading Dodgers, led by the tandem of John Lackey and Ben Weber. I'm surprised now as I write this that the trend of wearing Ben Weber-style athletic glasses hasn't swept the nation. They look considerably less nerdy now that Weber has a World Series ring.

Bank One Ballpark
San Francisco Giants @ Arizona Diamondbacks
July 5, 2002,
Section 306, Row 3, Seat 15

Now finished with California, I had one last stop to make before returning to New York. Following the Fourth of July holiday, I saw the Arizona Diamondbacks play twice against the Giants before the All-Star break. These games meant a lot in the standings, as the National League West was turning out to be a tight division.

The Diamondbacks were the defending World Series champions. After entering the league along with Tampa Bay in 1998, they became the fastest expansion team to reach the World Series, a record previously held by the 1997 Florida Marlins. As with the other Giants games, this series was nearly sold out by the time I arrived in the area. With their recent World Series win, the Diamondbacks had enjoyed predictable success at the box office this year. Arizonans were very proud of their champs.

The first things I noticed at Bank One Ballpark, or "the Bob," was how dark it was and how immense the crowds were. It clearly wasn't designed with traffic management in mind. I had read in press clippings that the Bob had a state-of-the-art ventilation system and was about as modern as a retractable-roof stadium could be. Downstairs it was freezing! I quickly forgot the 109-degree temperature outside and wished I had brought along another layer of clothing.

The Giants were taking batting practice, and I headed to the outfield to watch the show. Barry Bonds was up pretty quickly, and he hit one after another into the right-field seats. Balls bounced off the scoreboard, the screen, and several of the outfield signs. He finished as the pitchers moved into the outfield to begin their warm-up drills. The Giants trainer had them running and stretching before their throws. Most were following instructions, but Livan Hernandez was busy throwing balls to fans and generally doing his own thing, neglecting to participate in the team drill. Later, a couple of Giants fans mentioned how odd it was that he didn't seem to be focused on the game. Fans want to believe that the players care more about winning than anything else.

As expected, the fan base was made up mostly of folks who had migrated to Arizona from other parts of the country. The World Series victory against the Yankees had won the support of many fans who had moved there with allegiances to Eastern clubs. Yankee-hating baseball fans everywhere had cheered for the Diamondbacks, and the Phoenix team had become quite popular as the affable underdog.

I had timed my visit to Phoenix well, since I would see Curt Schilling pitch the first game and Randy Johnson pitch the second. I had never seen either in person, so I was excited. The match-up against the Giants couldn't have been better. Due to the scarcity of tickets I could only find a seat in the upper deck, and as soon as I arrived I was reminded that I was in Arizona. The cool climate they had created downstairs did not exist up here—it was scorching, and the air felt completely still. Curt Schilling pitched an outstanding complete game, challenging Bonds, who went 0 for 3 at the plate. Rich Aurilia was the only batter to get past first, hitting a home run in the ninth inning for only the fourth Giant hit.

In the second game, Johnson was equally impressive. Though Johnson did not come away with the victory, he struck out ten batters while giving up two runs on four hits in seven innings. The Giants won 3-2, with Bonds hitting a solo home run in the sixth.

Throughout this game, I had a little more time to pin down my feelings about the stadium. It was Luis Gonzales Bobblehead Day, and the stadium was a little nuttier than usual. To prevent fans from having to stand for hours in the Arizona sun, the Diamondbacks use a lottery system to give out the dolls. Arriving first does not give you any more of a chance of getting a doll than showing up after the first pitch. At the gate, everyone gets a scratch-and-win card. If yours says, "You're a Winner," you need to make your way to one of three locations to pick up your doll. The concourse was packed with people trying to figure out exactly where they needed to go. Even though it was a day game, the place seemed dark, and the atmosphere felt more like a prizefight than a baseball game, a feeling that was accentuated by the flashbulbs that exploded each time Bonds approached the plate. In the upper deck, I couldn't hear anything over the sound system, and the announcer sounded muffled. Downstairs the crowd seemed to be chattering about anything but the game.

The enclosed stadium offers one very marketable quality for Arizonians that isn't necessary in some other domed stadium cities—an air-conditioned environment. Here the casual observer may come to the park simply as an alternative way to escape the heat for a while. In doing so, they too may learn to love the game and before long become a seasoned fan. The stadium does not lend itself to the ideal baseball experience, but this may be one of the few locations where it probably doesn't need to. The regular follower of the game in Arizona has the opportunity to watch the professionals play both during the fall leagues and during spring training, when all the games are outdoors. This can provide those originally from other locales the opportunity to experience baseball played outdoors, like it was when they were kids, while Bank One provides them with their own unique air conditioned version.

My swing through the West Coast had come to a close. Now that I was half-finished with my trip, not only did I believe that I was going to be able to do it, but I was also starting to appreciate how much the fans' stories needed to be told. I returned home for the All-Star Game, looking forward to some rest and some time to collect my thoughts. Little did I know that during the second half of the season, a number of events would unfold that would make it more important than ever for the fans to tell their stories.

5

From a Game to a Business

As my understanding of the game changed and the discussion of a possible strike began heating up—even including some talk about players boycotting the All-Star Game—I became fascinated with how the business of baseball works. There are many issues facing the game today. In order to understand how we as fans can affect Major League Baseball, we first need to learn a little about the business of baseball and the factors that have shaped the game as we know it.

Leagues, Unions, and the Antitrust Exemption

Sometime in the mid-1800s, people began to play baseball in the Northeast United States. The rules varied depending on area, so in approximately 1865, Andrew Cartwright, Harry Chadwick, and a few others decided to standardize the rules of "Base Ball" to allow people from different regions to compete against one another. The game spread from the Northeast to other parts of the country by word of mouth, by travelers from the East along the railway lines. During the Civil War, northern troops introduced the game to the Southern regions, and by the end of the war baseball had taken hold in all corners of the country. Private clubs formed, and each town had its own team that would compete on weekends with teams from nearby communities.

Eventually, community sponsors began assisting the clubs, fencing off fields and adding stands so that teams could charge money for tickets. The players were all volunteers and would spend their weekdays working at full-time jobs. Eventually, friends of the clubs began offering full-time jobs to players in order to secure their loyalty to the team and to ensure that they would be available to play in any scheduled match-ups. Through this, the concept of the "ringer" was born.

In 1868, the president of the Cincinnati Baseball Club, Aaron Champion, realized that if he paid the players money to play baseball, they wouldn't have to work at their other jobs; they would not only be able to practice during the week, but they would also be available to travel for more distant matches. Certain players on others teams had most certainly been given stipends prior to this point (under the table, of course), but the Cincinnati Baseball Club was the first openly all-professional baseball team, and the first professional sports team in the United States. That first year, the entire team's payroll—there were only ten members on a team in those days—was $11,000. Eventually, high-caliber players from the East were lured to come and play for Cincinnati.

Though the team lost money in 1870 and the club was disbanded for a few years, the National League formed in 1871 with all professional teams. By 1879, the League had created the "reserve clause," which allowed a club to "reserve" its rights to five players to prevent richer clubs from signing the best players during the off-season. Competition for players had driven salaries up to unmanageable levels, and the teams with less revenue were training players and then losing them to larger markets with no compensation.

A rival league, the American Association, started up in 1882, advertising that it would not accept the reserve rule in the hope that it could entice players to leave the NL. This lasted for one season, and then it too set a five-player reserve. Over the next couple of years both leagues expanded the reserve clause to include eleven players, then fourteen, and then eventually every player on the roster. In 1885, members of the New York Giants formed a brotherhood that would stick together in order to make demands upon ownership. The brotherhood grew to include members throughout the league. When the league presidents refused to recognize the brotherhood, the members of this new "labor union" sought backers for their own league, which would begin play in 1889. They convinced 109 players from the two older leagues to jump over to the new Players League. With three leagues competing for fans, all of them lost money. Halfway through that season, several Players League clubs were forced to merge with the National League teams in their respective cities in order to avoid bankruptcy. The Players League collapsed, and the other two leagues swept in and gobbled up the athletes. When the National League team from Pittsburgh "stole" two players from the American Association, who had been left unprotected by the reserve clause, a war broke out. The agreement between the two leagues not to sign each other's players was declared void, and players again jumped from league to league indiscriminately. In 1891, the American Association again lost money and declared a truce. The two leagues merged, with four teams contracting and four others joining the National League.

A few years went by and the players again attempted to unionize, forming the Player's Protective Association (PPA). They asked for and received a meeting with the National League owners. The owners invited the press. Fearing negative publicity, both sides avoided all risk and accomplished little. In 1900, the league champion Brooklyn team received nothing extra for their efforts, no bonuses or raises, despite capturing the crown for the second consecutive year. The players' outrage prompted a second attempt by the players to find backing for another league. This led to the formation of the American League (AL) in 1901.

The American League immediately recognized the PPA, and they also promised to reserve players for no more than five years and to ask them for permission before trading them. This new league also allowed beer sales and play on Sundays, both of which were banned by the NL. Players again jumped leagues. Nap Lajoie, the Phillies star, signed with the new AL Philadelphia team, the Athletics. The Phillies took him to court and Lajoie's right to move was upheld—the court found that the contract was unbalanced since the team could terminate his employment with ten days' notice while he could not ever leave the Phillies as long as he was in baseball. Lajoie played the entire 1901 season for the Athletics before the Phillies' appeal was heard. The higher court ruled that since Lajoie had signed a contract agreeing to the terms, the contract was valid and Lajoie could not play for the A's. Since the case was heard in a Pennsylvania court, the American League leaders arranged for Lajoie to play for a team outside of Pennsylvania's jurisdiction. When his new team, the Indians, was scheduled to play the A's, Lajoie would simply take those days off.

The judge of the Pennsylvania Supreme Court set a precedent in this case that would have severe ramifications down the road. In the decision, he described baseball as a business "with a peculiar nature and circumstances." It was a "game, a sport," and as such, he decided, it should be treated differently than other types of businesses.[12]

In response to the success of the American League, several NL owners got together to develop strategies on how to win the war at the gates. The league would hire all of the managers and assign NL players to teams in a manner that would create the most revenue for the entire league, rather than allowing teams to obtain quality through trades and scouting. Simply, the big-market cities would be assigned the best players because the most money could be made there. Luckily, this idea died when the majority of owners couldn't be convinced to vote for it. None of the then "small market" teams fancied the prospect of losing out on premium talent for the benefit of the league.

The next plan was to lure away two big stars from the American League's Baltimore team with promises of high-paying managerial positions. These two stars, John McGraw and Joe Kelley, would have to sell their shares in the Orioles in order to accept the positions. Unbeknownst to them, they would be selling the shares to a representative of the National League. The new owners gave their unconditional release to every ballplayer wanted by a National League club. The head of the American League, Ban Johnson, called on the other AL clubs to send players to Baltimore immediately so the franchise would not forfeit a game and thereby lose its right to compete under league rules. The loss of one franchise would have meant the death of the eight-team league. The plan worked, and the team survived, but the replacement players were not strong athletes and the Orioles soon became an unprofitable club—and thus a candidate for relocation. In 1903, the Baltimore Orioles moved to New York and were renamed the Highlanders, and eventually the New York Yankees. In 1902, the National League, having taken a beating at the box office in every market, made peace with the American League, mostly on the American League's terms. The American League, not needing the ballplayers on its side any longer, adopted the reserve clause. The ballplayers once again lost what little leverage they had gained.

In 1913, the Federal League (FL) was formed. Although it was originally supposed to be a minor league, later that year it announced it would draw talent away from the major-league franchises and compete on their level—and in many of the same cities. The increase in pay for the few who jumped leagues led to massive migrations over following years, and the original major-league clubs began blacklisting players and suing them to prevent further defections. The Federal Baseball League then sued MLB to prevent them from blocking access to their talent, claiming unfair restraint of trade. Judge Kennesaw Mountain Landis, who heard the case, decided to review it, hoping that the two sides would settle, which they did. Prior to that though, Landis declared, "I am shocked, because you call playing baseball 'labor.'" The Federal League franchises were soon absorbed into the other two leagues or bought out. The one exception was the new Baltimore franchise, whose owner refused to accept the meager offer for his club and filed his own anti-trust suit against MLB.

Antitrust legislation had recently come to pass in Congress, and the country as a whole was supportive of the breakup of so-called monopolies. Baltimore won the first round in court but lost on appeal, with the court stating, "The players travel from place to place in interstate commerce, but they are not the game...which is local in its beginning and in its end." The fact that the owners made a profit seemed irrelevant. "They are still sport and not trade." Justice Oliver Wendell Holmes heard the next round of appeals and argued that the games occurred entirely within the jurisdiction of the state, and that the crossing of state lines is "a mere incident, not the essential thing." He went on to add, "Personal effort, not related to production, is not a subject of commerce." This was known as the Federal Baseball Decision and has been the basis for the anti-trust exemption that baseball enjoys to this day. Since baseball was not considered trade, the reserve clause, whereby players could be held to one team for life, couldn't be a restraint-of-trade issue.[13]

Baseball Gets a Commissioner

The next significant change in how baseball operated occurred in 1919. The Chicago White Sox and Cincinnati Reds were to face each other in the World Series that year. This was the first non-wartime season in five years, and attendance for all the clubs had been the highest ever. For this reason, owners decided to revert to the original best-of-nine series format from the recent best-of-seven.

Several players on the White Sox had been promised bonuses for meeting benchmarks in their respective areas of expertise that season. Ownership reneged, however. The most well known example is that of Eddie Cicotte, who was promised a $10,000 bonus if he won thirty games in 1919. After his twenty-ninth win, management sat him for two weeks so he could "rest for the Series," thereby costing him the opportunity to win his thirtieth game. Additionally, the Sox owner, Charlie Comiskey, promised the team a bonus if they won the pennant. Following the clinching game, though, the players discovered that the bonus was simply one case of champagne to share among them.

Gangsters and racketeers had always been a problem in baseball. Although it was widely believed that many players took money to throw a game here and there, no one thought that fixing the World Series was possible. The disgruntled state of the players on the White Sox may have made it possible for the gamblers to do just that. The money that was offered was considerable, and eight members of the team (six fielders and two pitchers), still upset that they hadn't received their promised bonuses, agreed to throw the Series. After the Series began, the gangsters, unable to come up with the second cash installment, reneged on their deal, figuring that the players were in no position to complain. In response, the team started playing to win again. The gangsters retaliated, approaching one member of the team and threatening the lives of him and his wife, likely leading to his collapse in the final game.

In their attempts to gather enough money to execute the fix, the racketeers had informed many people about the plan. As word spread throughout Chicago, newspapermen began reporting the story and several of the White Sox team members were called to testify before a grand jury. The remaining individuals involved were implicated by this testimony and brought to trial. The case was thrown out for lack of evidence, although many believe it was a sham to begin with. The damage had been done, however, and baseball's image suffered greatly from the scandal. Baseball was supposed to be able to regulate itself, but in the eyes of the public it was clearly not doing a very good job.

Owners, feeling they needed to make a statement to restore the game's lost integrity, created the position of commissioner of baseball. They approached Federal Judge Kennesaw Mountain Landis to fill the position. Judge Landis had a reputation for being a tough trustbuster and a man of high morality. His appointment would send a signal to the country that baseball was now above reproach and that any notion of baseball being a big business—like Standard, Oil for example—was unfounded, as Landis was known to be intolerant of monopolies. Judge Landis had one criterion for accepting the position: he insisted that it be a position for life, and that the owners could never fire him. They would have to give him full power to operate the two leagues as he saw fit.

The owners agreed, eager to have such a forthright man represent them and certain that he would always agree that their best interests were also the best interests of baseball. His first action was to ban the eight bribe-takers for life, saying, "Regardless of the verdict of the juries, no player who throws a ball game, no player who undertakes or promises to throw a ball game, no player who sits in confidence with a bunch of crooked players and does not promptly tell his club about it, will ever play professional baseball."

Despite Landis's strict nature, in 1927, when Ty Cobb and Tris Speaker, two of baseball's biggest heroes, were implicated for fixing games back in 1919, Landis merely moved them to other teams. The two players were too popular to ban, and Landis waved off criticism by saying that the infraction had occurred prior to his appointment.[13]

Judge Landis governed the two leagues until his death in 1944. Former U.S. Senator A. B. "Happy" Chandler replaced Landis, but the owners soon regretted the appointment. They had originally chosen him because they thought they could easily control him, but they soon saw this wouldn't be the case, and that his definition of the "best interests of baseball" did not always coincide with that of the owners. He was removed from the post in 1951 and replaced with NL President Ford Frick. By this time, it was clearly apparent that the commissioner was merely an extension of ownership and not the impartial arbitrator originally conceived.

The Great Migration

The next substantial shift in the status quo of baseball occurred in 1953, when the Boston Braves moved their team to Milwaukee to a brand-new municipally-funded stadium. This move was significant for a number of reasons. Though teams had moved frequently throughout baseball's early years, no one had moved in nearly half a century. However, the teams now realized two things: first, they needed to follow the population shift in order to maximize their profits, and, second, in order to lure a team to a new locale, cities would finance a state-of-the-art facility for them to play in. No longer did an owner need to weigh the virtues of spending his own money to rebuild or refurbish his stadium to keep up with the status quo. Now an owner could simply threaten to leave the city for another if his stadium wasn't properly maintained.

Competition ensued between cities to lure teams away. The Braves had not been terribly popular in Boston, so their loss was not a terrible blow to the city. However, when the Dodgers and Giants moved west a few years later, just two years after the Dodgers had won the World Series, the trend went into full swing. The Dodger exodus in particular was devastating to Brooklyn fans and proved that owners had no loyalty to the people who had brought them success in the past.

Milwaukee discovered this pain itself when the Braves, just thirteen years after migrating from Boston, jumped ship again and moved to Atlanta, who had financed and built a stadium for them. With the new park in place and the possibility of lucrative television rights on the horizon, the Braves' owner, who had previously shown no loyalty to Boston, now turned his back on Milwaukee.

Tampa Bay built Tropicana Field only a decade ago in an attempt to lure the White Sox, the Mariners, and finally the Giants to Florida. In order to stabilize the baseball landscape, and to put an end to any lingering lawsuits over the city's inability to draw a team, MLB expanded, granting a franchise to Tampa Bay.[14]

When the San Francisco Giants were put up for sale, an ownership group presented plans to buy the team and move them to Florida. The plan was rejected by MLB, and local businessmen purchased the Giants for less money than the Florida owners group had offered. The new owners tried to find public funding for a new stadium, but when that proved impossible, they were able to find private backers. This was the first time an ownership group had managed to do so since the Braves moved to Milwaukee.

The private financing of the Giants' new stadium does not represent a new trend, however. Rather, contraction seems to be the new card that MLB has up its sleeve to get communities to finance new facilities. It has worked in Minnesota, where a levy has passed to build a new stadium for the Twins.

MLB refuses to allow municipalities to own franchises for fear that politicians—who come and go regularly, each with their own agendas—will affect the game's stability. They also may wish to avoid exposing the private dealings of MLB to the public. If a city assumed a percentage of ownership, it would have a say in the team's movement. However, without the ability to purchase their team, the city has little recourse but to build a new stadium if it wishes to retain its franchise (and thus maintain its national civic profile). MLB's policy to keep municipalities out of ownership positions is clearly an antitrust issue, since it is a restraint of trade, but, without action by National lawmakers, nothing will change.

Challenges to the Federal Baseball Decision

The same year that the Braves moved to Milwaukee, the reserve clause would be contended in the courts once again. George Toolson refused to honor his reserve clause and sued the Yankees under the Sherman Act, claiming restraint of trade. When the case arrived on the Supreme Court's doorstep, it decided to let the Federal Baseball ruling stand. They based their decision on the fact the Congress had not attempted to remove baseball's exemptions in the previous thirty years, which, the Court decided, amounted to a tacit approval of them. The Court also said that baseball had developed under the understanding that it was exempt, and that for the Court to change its mind about the matter now would create a chaotic business situation.

MLB now had reason to believe it was safe from all antitrust suits. In 1959, MLB, to demonstrate its newfound security, announced that it would welcome a third league. New York Mayor John Lindsay, having just lost both the Dodgers and the Giants, convinced New York businessman William Shea to back the new league. MLB and the new Continental League (CL) began negotiating the terms of their cohabitation. When they reached an impasse, it again seemed as though the antitrust exemption would be challenged in court. However, the CL fell apart when MLB offered to add franchises in four of the new league's prospective cities. MLB's expansion had begun.

Unionization

The formation of the National Labor Relations Board (NLRB) in 1935 demonstrated a new attitude towards labor issues in the United States. This organization, which would oversee labor practices, gave new ammunition to those wishing to collectively bargain. This would be the most significant legislation ever to assist the players in their plight against management.

The players attempted to unionize in 1946, but ownership was able to thwart the effort by creating a pension plan and raising the minimum salary. It was in fact major-league umpires who were the first to use the NLRB successfully, when the board ruled it had jurisdiction on several grounds. First, organized baseball relied on a commissioner for self-regulation, and as the commissioner was hired and could be fired by ownership, he would unlikely be impartial in any attempts to resolve disputes. Second, the board found that ownership was inaccurate when it described umpires as "supervisors," a non-labor classification that would prevent them from forming a union. This decision by the board would also allow the Major League Baseball Players Association, created in 1962, to negotiate the handling of the players' pension fund under collective bargaining. Many players felt strongly that they didn't want to form an actual union. Fearing repercussions from their clubs, many toed the line, claiming the reserve clause was actually necessary for baseball to exist. They hired an owner-friendly lawyer to represent them in the pension-fund negotiations.

By 1966, the tide had shifted, however, and the players wanted a full-time representative. The committee turned to Marvin Miller, a successful labor-law expert who had assisted the United Steelworkers Union. Owners began to worry. Miller spent time educating the players about the benefits of collective bargaining, but he did not manage to win all of them over. That same year, however, Don Drysdale and Sandy Koufax decided to not sign their contracts unless the two of them received substantial raises. It worked, as they were both key members of the Dodgers team. Soon after, even the skeptical players saw the benefits of collective bargaining and began to follow Miller's lead. Ownership squawked, even blacklisting Robin Roberts, who had been instrumental in hiring Miller. The players saw this act as the final straw, and now Miller had little difficulty bringing the rank and file into line. Baseball's first labor agreement came together in January 1968. It was a one-year agreement that raised the minimum salary and gave the players the right to hire agents to represent them. It also established a grievance procedure that would allow the commissioner to arbitrate grievances for players who had at least three years of major-league experience. The owners refused to come to an agreement with the MLBPA the following year, thinking they might be able to break the union. In response, the players did not show up for spring training camps. Ownership quickly knuckled under and came to an agreement, increasing their contributions to the pension fund. Bowie Kuhn, who was instrumental in the agreement, was appointed the new commissioner.

In October 1969, Curt Flood was traded from the Cardinals seemingly because of personal differences with the ownership. He asked the commissioner to intercede on his behalf, since he had been with the Cardinals for over ten years and felt he should have some say in his future. Commissioner Kuhn refused to help, and Flood refused to go to the new club, first announcing his retirement and then declaring himself a free agent. The commissioner refused to acknowledge his declaration. Having no other recourse, Flood filed suit in December against Major League Baseball in the hope that that he would gain the right to negotiate his own contract with the new club. With the NLRB ruling that it had jurisdiction over the umpires just months earlier, MLB became concerned that if the case went to court, the commissioner would not meet the test as an impartial arbitrator. No club would sign Flood, since the commissioner's office did not view him as a free agent, so he sat out a year. The following season, his rights were traded again, and he agreed to play for his new team, the Washington Senators, as long as his agreement would have no effect on the outcome of his lawsuit. Having sat out a year, though, his skills had faded. In the end, Flood lost his case, and also his career, but his suit had a very important effect on the sport. In the collective bargaining agreement (CBA) of 1970, MLB agreed to the appointment of an impartial arbitrator to settle all contract disputes, fearing they might lose their antitrust exemption if a repeat of the Flood incident occurred.

In 1972, the owners were still hesitant about bargaining with the players, thinking that perhaps that if they refused to negotiate the union might collapse. This led to another strike, and again the owners settled by increasing their contribution to the pension fund, this time by $500,000. Though the nine-day strike had cost the players $600,000, they had made one very big gain: they had proved they would stick together, while the owners hadn't.

The reserve clause, which guaranteed the automatic one year renewal of a player's contract at the previous year's terms, was still in effect. In 1975, Andy Messersmith and Dave McNally, who had both been unable to come to a new agreement with their clubs, played an entire year without a contract. They took their grievance to the arbitrator, who declared them free agents. From then on, baseball—and baseball players—would never be the same. Players could now negotiate their contracts on equal footing with management. In addition, after six years on the major league clubs 40-man roster, a player could automatically become a free agent. Also, the players obtained the right to veto a trade if they had ten years of major-league experience and five years with their current team, much as Flood had wanted to do.

After the decision in the Toolson case, the courts asked Congress to clear up the confusion. Other sports have not been granted the exemption that baseball has, yet Congress refuses to clarify the issue. Often it comes up for discussion when a team threatens to move or a when a senator wants to lean on MLB in order to obtain an expansion franchise for his constituents. It also comes up when the sport experiences a period of labor unrest. As soon as either issue is resolved, though, antitrust is placed on the backburner once again.

If the exemption were lifted, MLB would be open to legal disputes in many areas—from players, cities, and potential owners. They could also be audited, meaning they would have to share their books with the MLBPA. The exemption has served one important purpose, limiting team movement, since it is ultimately the commissioner who makes decisions regarding franchise relocation. However, if cities could stipulate that a percentage of the team be turned over to them before they built new stadiums, perhaps the need for a commissioner to regulate movement wouldn't be necessary.

Effects of Free Agency

In 1975, Catfish Hunter was declared a free agent because Charley Finley, the owner of the Athletics, failed to pay half of Hunter's salary into a life-insurance fund, as stipulated in his contract. The Yankees, seeing an opportunity to snag one of the greatest pitchers in baseball, signed him to a $3.5 million contract, which was significantly larger than any other at the time. Seeing the possibilities of free agency, many players began refusing to sign contracts, opting instead to become free agents to find out just how much they could make on the open market. Teams, who always want the best players available, offered more and more money, until salaries became exorbitant.

Arbitration was the next big concession the MLBPA won. A player with three years' experience who was not eligible for free agency could now have his contract determined by an independent arbitrator if he was in the top percentage of players at his position. With arbitrators from outside the baseball world now deciding the worth of young players, based on various statistical comparisons to experienced veterans, salaries began to skyrocket. The main problem with the arbitration system, which has never been remedied, was that the people deciding the cases were given only two salary numbers: one submitted by the player and one by the club. The arbitrators had to, and still must, choose one of these two numbers and could not split the difference. If the arbitrator determined that the player was worth more than the salary offered by the club the player received the higher number. Agents, always aware of where their young and talented clients rank, took full advantage of the system, entering extremely high dollar amounts and pointing to the lucrative free-agent contracts of veteran players. If a shortstop one year got a certain number, then a better shortstop the next year would ask for significantly more, knowing there was a good chance he would get it.

Though a few teams over the years have been guilty of giving out extraordinarily large contracts to free agents, it is actually the escalating victories in arbitration that have pushed up player salaries. A vicious circle is created: First, a young player receives a high salary due to arbitration. Then, a highly skilled veteran feels he is more valuable than this kid who has received such a large award, and so he demands more on the free agent market. Then another player argues that he is younger, with less wear and tear, than that veteran and deserves more money since his best years are ahead of him. Thus, the salaries climb higher and higher.

These days, the best player on the market is treated like the best player ever, a phenomenon Mike Lupica wrote about in his book *Mad as Hell*. It's the reason that Mike Hampton, who in 2000 won fifteen games, was offered $15 million to play in Colorado the next season. The Bob Fellers and Bob Gibsons of the world should be angry when a guy starts earning $1 million dollars a win just because there are a limited number of free-agent pitchers available and Colorado wants to entice the best one out there to come play for them.

Also, because the arbitration cases are binding, teams have less control over their total payroll. In order to keep an Andruw Jones, the winner of the largest arbitration case in history, a team might have to trade away another star player to balance the payroll. Arbitration handcuffs the clubs, particularly those with little payroll flexibility.

The 2002 Collective Bargaining Agreement

The 2002 CBA took steps to curtail excessive spending by clubs by creating a luxury tax. After years of trying unsuccessfully to get a salary cap, owners pushed for a tax that would act as a soft ceiling. The luxury tax works as follows: A payroll limit is set, and if teams spend more than that limit, they are taxed at a steep rate on the amount above that line, with the tax dollars going to the commissioner's discretionary fund. The off-season following the agreement saw a marked turnaround in free-agent spending, with some big names getting large salaries and many middle-of-the-road players taking a pay cut.

Frank Thomas, the designated hitter for the Chicago White Sox, was released from his contract on grounds of "diminished skills"; he then, signed a new incentive-laden contract with the same team. This could be a sign that things are turning around. People in Chicago like Frank Thomas. He's a White Sox persona that fans are familiar with and would like to see remain around—but not at top dollar when he is performing only slightly above average for a player in his position. The compromise was a way to maintain continuity with team's past by giving a fan favorite one more chance while acting fiscally responsibly. Thomas was able to return to good form in 2003.

Teams in smaller markets and those who are rebuilding can benefit from keeping the local fan favorite around a little longer. With fans needing scorecards to keep up with the changes on the field, having one player remain a constant presence cannot be overrated. Players also want stability, which is why they seek out long-term deals. Teams are willing to pay long-term deals to valuable players for two reasons. First, a quality starter's skills in the short-term might be worth any problems that could arise over the length of the long contract. Second, a long-term deal might end up being cheaper in the long run than several shorter deals strung together, since arbitration is always a danger, and the free agent market is difficult to forecast. The new CBA will probably make long-term deals much less desirable for clubs as they learn that they need to remain flexible with their payroll over the long term. Also, the companies that insure contracts limit their coverage to three years, so if a career-ending injury occurs in the later years of a long-term contract, the team receives no compensation.

Major League Baseball now permits clubs to carry only a certain percentage of their value as debt. This is an old rule, but is has not been enforced for years. This rule, along with the luxury tax, limits spending by clubs that don't have the ability to generate a lot of revenue and keeps clubs from bidding up on short-term contracts with the idea of paying the debt off later. Clubs that have less debt of course can afford to spend more money on players and other personnel without endangering their long-term fiscal viability. This rule creates a drag on salaries, but its main goal is to ensure the financial stability of every team.

Free agency is part of baseball, and it is actually a good part. Anyone should have the right to negotiate for their services, and if that brings them untold amounts of money, so be it. Though it does create more player movement, it allows teams to fortify areas on their rosters that may have been weakened by injury or poor amateur scouting. It also requires the front-office management to be more accountable to the fans for the product on the field.

For fans, the key to understanding free agency is to take a comprehensive view of all of the decisions that make up a trade or signing before we decide the value of it. We can only decide weather we value the overall product that the team puts forth. Do we enjoy our time at the park? Do we care about the team and how they play the game? If we find that we no longer enjoy our experience at the ballpark, we need to determine why, and in a reasonable manner voice our concerns to the club. Only through a real understanding of our team's state of affairs can we decide whether they deserve our loyalty or not.

Media Rights

Let's add one more thing into the equation. In this time of free agency, revenue generated through television rights and advertising is more important than ever to ensure costs can be met. Simply, if a team has more television viewers, advertisers will pay television networks more to run their ads during the game, and networks will pay teams more for programming rights. The more people that are in the stands, the more money the team can get for stadium naming rights and in-game sponsorship.

There are two types of television deals. First, there is the package deal negotiated by MLB, where a network pays money to the league, which is then shared equally among the teams. The two parties designate a specific number of games, played on specific days.

MLB has two packages. One is with ESPN for games every Sunday night and twice during the week, as well as several games of the Division Series round of the playoffs. The ESPN package provides teams with national exposure to cable subscribers—possibly in distant markets they would otherwise not reach. Those who live in very rural areas with no access to pay television or who cannot afford cable will not be able to see these games, however.

The second package is with FOX, which broadcasts Saturday afternoon games throughout the season, the All-Star Game, a certain number of playoff games in each of the first two rounds, and the entire World Series. FOX is the only network that offers national broadcasts throughout the year on regular commercial television. However, they carry them only on Saturday afternoons, when young people are likely to be involved in their own sporting pursuits; also, to maximize its audience it exposes regional markets to the same teams each week. During the playoffs, the games are scheduled to start during prime television viewing hours to reap the most advertising dollars, often pushing the games late into the night, when school-aged children are in bed.

The second type of television deal is made directly with the individual clubs for the rights to broadcast any games not included in the league package. These often go to regional sports networks, which are also on cable, again resulting in limiting viewership. In cities with large populations like New York and Los Angeles, the price for these rights is much higher. This accounts for the large discrepancies in revenue between large- and small-market teams. A percentage of each local club's television contract is also paid into a central league fund, which in turn pays out to small-market clubs that need financial help. Some teams make an additional arrangement to broadcast a handful of games on a local commercial network, but those are becoming fewer and fewer, as local affiliates cannot afford to pay as much as the dedicated sports channels. The monthly cable fee may also preclude at least one visit to the park for a live game, as the costs for each are roughly the same.

The Cubs and the Braves both have their own dedicated stations that broadcast nationally. These teams with the so-called Superstations pay an extra fee into the central fund, as they are able to broadcast not only in their own territory but also in the territories of other teams. These teams, as well as others, such as the Red Sox, who also share ownership with the New England Sports Network (NESN), and the Yankees, who own the YES network, have another advantage. Because the team owns the network, the network can buy the rights to air the team's games for less than market value. This benefits the network, since they receive guaranteed content that attracts large advertising dollars while paying little for it. The team benefits by having lower television contracts, thereby paying less into the central pool and sharing less with its competitors. When teams say they are losing money, it is often because they have found ways to pay revenue to another company that they also own. The Yes network collects large dividends from advertisers that want to be associated with Yankee broadcasts, but because the Yes Network can pay below-market fees to the team, this profit isn't passed along to the Yankee's books. Since the owner of both the network and the team is the same, they reap the benefit regardless of whether the team appears to turn a profit.

This isn't really a new practice. Many beer companies purchased teams in order to take advantage of free advertising and to have a venue where they could sell their product exclusively. In the past Budweiser's profits didn't go to the St. Louis Cardinals but rather into the Anheuser-Busch coffers. The difference of course, is the amount of money involved. Where it was thousands in Gussie Busch's time, now it's millions and tens of millions. Small-market teams will never have the ability to create their own networks, because they won't be able to draw enough advertisers to pay the bills, let alone take advantage of all of the benefits of underselling those rights. They also lose out because of the smaller fees the big-market teams pay as a result of owning their own networks.

Another reason why securing television rights has become more important than filling seats is that most teams do not own their own stadiums, parking lots, or concessions. Some teams, like the Twins, rent the venue from the local football team (which, in the Vikings' case, makes a profit on each Metro dog sold during Twins games). Likewise, the city of Los Angeles controls the parking lot outside of Dodger Stadium. The team usually controls its ticket prices, but not always its vendor's prices. We blame the team when the cost of a beer goes up, but often it is someone else who is taking advantage of the fan's willingness to pay for it. Though it seems that the average TV viewer, who pays a couple of dollars a month to get the cable channel that shows his team's games, is contributing much less than the guy in the stands who pays for a ticket, a couple of hot dogs, a couple of beers, parking, and a program, that fan may be contributing to the team only through the purchase of the ticket and the program. Thus, teams need to be creative to find the revenue they need to remain competitive, let alone turn a profit.

We need advertisers to believe that if the stadium isn't full, no one is watching at home. We need to make both teams and advertisers think of the fans in the stands as the people who generate the publicity for the team. There is no better publicity than 40,000 people going home from a game and telling their friends what a great experience they had. If 40,000 people do that every day for all eighty-one home games, that will account for more than 3.2 million people walking through the turnstiles and at least as many at home wishing they had also been there. We need to let advertisers on non-pay television as well as companies that sponsor in-stadium promotions know that we like what they are doing. We can buy their products, and we can write them to let them know. Also, if a team is advertising on television or in the park in a way that lessens our enjoyment of the game, then we also need to let them know. We can control our experience in the ballpark by speaking out to those companies that do batter us with ads. Most companies have websites with feedback forms to make the process simple. They want to hear positive feedback. One written letter is estimated to represent approximately 20,000 people, so just by taking a few moments we can let our voices be heard loud and clear.

6

Circling the Bases: Part III

I used the All-Star break in 2002 as many of the players did, as an opportunity to rest for the second half of the season. I expected the All-Star Game itself to be uneventful, as it had grown less and less exciting over the past few years. Interleague play, the consolidation of National League and American League umpires into one body, and free agency had made the need to see the leagues compete much less important.

In the days just before the game, I began to hear rumblings that some players voted into the starting lineup were planning not to attend. Many expressed the desire to spend time with family or simply to rest. In a season I had spent talking to fans about the joy they received from baseball, I was disgusted by this news. Though wanting to rest so they can be ready to fight through the rest of the season may seem like a legitimate reason for players to skip the game, the point of the All-Star Game is to provide players and fans with an opportunity to honor each other. It should be looked upon as a command performance. The time off shouldn't serve as a reward; in fact, baseball should consider using this entire week as a way to say "thank you" to fans everywhere. Each stadium could plan activities for local supporters, ones that involve players who aren't invited to All-Star events. If a player voted onto the team doesn't want to play, he should have to be on the disabled list in order to miss it, and even then he should still have to attend some of the festivities. If they don't show up, they should be fined by MLB. It's the commissioner's job to do what's in the best interest of baseball; ensuring that the fans' voices are respected, by ensuring that they get to see the players they voted for perform in the All-Star Game, is definitely in the game's best interests.

Public relations problems at the Midsummer Classic have not been limited to no-shows, however. The game has been deteriorating in terms of competitive quality since 1970, when Pete Rose slid into Ray Fosse while trying to score, injuring Fosse's shoulder. Rose was criticized for playing so hard during a game that "didn't count." The 2002 All-Star game, halted in the eleventh inning because both teams had used up all of their pitchers, was the ultimate game that "didn't count." No one went to this game either imagining that they might see a player get injured, nor even expecting to see every player play, but what they got was significantly more disappointing. The joy of watching a Schilling or a Glavine pitch can't really be appreciated in one inning over three at-bats. Watching Glavine find his spots and nibble at the corners throughout the entire game is part of the magic. Just like watching Torii Hunter steal the homer away from Barry Bonds, the chance to see pitchers work in their own style is part of the reason we are there. There is an argument to be made for allowing fans to see each player who has made the trip to the All-Star Game, but more than anything, they want to see a *quality* exhibition, and they want to see their side win. The Yankees wouldn't have the fans that they do if they didn't win. If the All-Star game is going to continue to draw any interest at all, the fans need to feel that it matters to the people on the field. Also, baseball is the game without a clock. The managers should play with that in mind. Bob Brenley and Joe Torre should have realized much earlier than they apparently did that they needed to plan for extra innings.

If MLB wants the game simply to be a showcase, it needs to stop marketing it as a battle between the leagues. They should make it a fun way to get the fans involved in the game and to generate publicity for the sponsors. For example, two different sponsors could hold a contest to pick fans that want to be the thirtieth man. They could select five men each to audition on Homerun-Derby Day to pitch the last inning of the game. The fan chosen would get to sit on the bench and, in the event of a tie game, pitch an inning. As non-professionals, they would probably give up enough hits that the game would be left up to the fielders. Another idea would be to bring back former all-stars, in the same manner that they choose the honorary captains. These "old-timers" could give fans a thrill for an inning or two. If one wants to call it a battle, though, no matter what, there must be a winner.

In 2003 and 2004, the game was played to determine home-field advantage in the World Series. Though this isn't the best solution, it does show that MLB is opening its eyes to the problem. The game itself doesn't mean enough to the players. It is difficult to believe that the representative from the Tigers or Tampa Bay is going to care who has home-field advantage for the World Series, but it is a start. Recognizing that this is a business, the winners of the All-Star game should get a share of the gate. The next step is to put a clause in players' contracts giving them a bonus if they make the team and fining them a larger amount if they make the team but refuse to participate. The players that come should fulfill their obligations as they would on their own club. The only player that should be guaranteed to play as a reserve is the sole representative of the club that is hosting the event.

The 2002 All-Star Game should be remembered as the game where the fans began to rebel. That the game ended in a tie shows that the focus of the event was not the game itself but the opportunity to make money from sponsors. Everything was planned, except what to do in the case of a tie ballgame. I suppose Bud Selig and MLB thought the fans at the game wouldn't care, that they were there as guests of large corporations, or had won contests and didn't really follow baseball. What we all found out is the fans at that game were like fans at all games—they wanted a team to root for, a team to identify with, a team to be proud of, and they wanted to win. Sportswriter Dick Young, quoted in *The Sporting News* in May 1969, said, "If you were to walk into a ballpark...to watch two teams...that you had no rooting interest in whatsoever, chances are you would walk out in the middle. It is the rooting interest that keep the millions excited in baseball...That is baseball's great strength."[15] I imagine that is how the unruly fans in Milwaukee felt when they lost their chance to root.

Olympic Stadium
Atlanta Braves @ Montreal Expos
July 13, 2002,

The first game I attended after the All-Star break took place in one of the cities that had caused me to start this journey. The Montreal Expos had finished last in fan attendance for the past seven years. It was also a team whose primary owner seemed to have bailed out, by selling the franchise back to MLB and the other twenty-nine teams in order to purchase the Marlins and start over. Omar Minaya, the new general manager appointed by MLB, had just pulled off an amazing pair of trades. First he traded with Cleveland for Bartolo Colon, as mentioned earlier, and then he traded to get outfielder Cliff Floyd from Florida.

Up to this point, the National League East had been a closely contested division, and the Expos were actually in contention midway through the season. The Expos were playing above expectations, while the Braves and Mets were playing far below. Minaya had made the trades in the hope of making a run at the playoffs. I arrived in Montreal the day after Floyd had made his debut and just in time to see Bartolo Colon's first game. Again, I would see the Braves play on the road. With great anticipation I bought a ticket, thrilled about the prospect of seeing Colon versus Glavine.

As I filed into Olympic Stadium, or the "Big O" as it is sometimes called, along with 17,334 other people, I was aghast at what I saw. It was dark and dirty. My neighbor, originally from Montreal, had said that sitting in Olympic Stadium was like sitting in the bottom of a toilet. I agreed, although I would add "in a truck stop along a little-used highway." The place felt filthy. Originally built to host the 1976 Olympics, and not baseball, it felt like a makeshift solution for a team that had found itself at the last minute without a place to play. Unfortunately, the Expos had been playing here for twenty-five years. Jokes had been made about George Steinbrenner buying the Expos and being allowed to run them, just to see what a difference ownership would make. I would like to have seen that, because I believe that even the Yankees couldn't have drawn 20,000 people to that stadium. The Big O was, in my mind, the worst place ever to watch a baseball game.

Had I come to see the Expos later in the season, I probably wouldn't remember a thing about the game. The dull, dim surroundings would have suited a team that had given up, as they seemed to do by the end of August, and the experience would have been miserable. But on this day, the place was filled with more hope than I had ever seen at a baseball game. Not only were the Expos doing well, but the general manager seemed to believe they could compete. He also seemed to care! He was trading for players that the Expos would have traded away to contenders in the past by the midseason mark. Omar Minaya had managed to create the most magical thing a GM can create: hope.

The fans were cheering and singing French songs. Everyone was smiling at the new stars wearing their Expos uniforms. The new acquisitions didn't disappoint either. Colon pitched a complete-game shutout against the Atlanta Braves. He did get into trouble once, and it looked like he might not make it, but after that inning, he returned to form and kept on delivering heat. To make it even sweeter for Expos fans, Glavine was not having a good night. After struggling through the first inning, Glavine seemed to regain his form, working efficiently until the fifth. Then, Brad Wilkerson stepped into the batter's box and hit the ball out of the park. Jose Vidro followed and grounded out to third. Then Vladimer Guererro also stroked one out of the park, followed by Cliff Floyd, who did the same. Fernando Tatis walked and then stole second. Galarraga struck out. Cabrerra singled to right, scoring Tatis, and then Glavine walked Michael Barrett. Glavine left the game, and Tim Spooneybarger came in to pitch to Colon, who bunted back to the pitcher. The Braves relievers did their job the rest of the night, but Colon's win was assured. Final score: 6 to 3.

As I walked out of the ballpark, I was caught in a current of excited fans, who sang and cheered all the way home. Hope had returned to Montreal, and the joyous tones of the songs they were singing lifted my spirits. I left feeling like baseball would return to this city and the stadium would begin to fill. I was hopeful that MLB would remain there, that the fans would show Selig that the game could survive if people that cared ran it. An organization had formed—Save Our 'Spos—to help keep the team there. Fans who had been avoiding the team in protest were suddenly looking for any means possible to show their support. Unfortunately for Montreal, the rest of the National League East awoke following the All-Star break and began playing solid baseball. The Braves pulled ahead, and it was clear that the Expos weren't going to give anyone a run for it this year.

Because of salary limitations imposed by the Expos owners (namely, the owners of the other twenty-nine clubs), Minaya would have to trade away some of the team's talent or lose them to free agency in the off-season. MLB had set the Expos up for failure by severely limiting the team's payroll, placing them in the lowest echelon of major-league teams. If Omar Minaya had been allowed to maintain the average salary of the other twenty-nine teams instead, the Expos not only would have been able to retain some of the players who had brought hope to Montreal on this night, but they also would have been able to compete in the off-season market. In 2003 and 2004, they played six weeks in Puerto Rico in order to draw fans from the area to professional baseball and to boost revenue for the struggling franchise. Then MLB announced the team would move to the Washington, D.C., area for the 2005 season. They did so too late, however, for the team to plan any kind of closing ceremony for the final game in Montreal, missing an opportunity to maintain any warm thoughts in the minds of Montreal baseball fans.

The franchise was born in 1969 when the NL expanded. More than 100,000 fans greeted players for a parade the team threw before the home opener. Two weeks after beginning play, Bill Stoneman pitched the team's first no-hitter, a feat he would repeat three years later. Originally playing in Jarry Park, which held less than 28,500, the team managed to pass the 1 million mark that first season. In 1973, they contended for the division for most of the season. In 1977, Olympic Stadium opened, with an attendance of 57,592 for the first game. In 1979, the team again finished strongly, behind the Pittsburgh Pirates, and the following year they came second behind the Philadelphia Phillies. In both years, the division win came down to the final series. During the strike-shortened 1981 season, the team finished with league's best second-half record and won the playoff series, beating the Phillies for their first division title. They lost in the NLCS to the Dodgers.

In 1994, the Expos would set a midweek-series attendance record when they beat the Braves and took over first place in their division. Again, the season would be shortened by a strike, but the team ended up with the best record in baseball, six games ahead of the Braves. Pedro Martinez came up in 1995 and in 1997 won the team's first Cy Young with a 1.90 ERA and 305 strikeouts in 206.2 innings pitched. Vladimir Guererro became the first Expo to hit more than forty home runs in one season in 1999.

In 2001, the sale of the Montreal Expos by Jeffery Loria to the other twenty-nine owners of MLB was approved, as was the sale of the Marlins to Loria. Only three years prior to 1998 did the team finish with less than 1 million fans in attendance, and in all three the team finished either fifth or sixth in their division. The falloff that began in 1998, then, cannot be contributed merely to disinterest; rather, it was a reaction to what was happening in baseball and with the Expos ownership at the time. The team finished last in attendance in 2002 only because of a last-minute move by the Marlins, now under Jeff Loria, to purchase all unsold tickets on the final weekend to avoid that distinction.

It is important to understand the timing of the purchase of the Montreal franchise. What happens to the value of a losing franchise purchased for $150 million by MLB in the same season that the Boston Red Sox are purchased for $700 million? The Boston Red Sox franchise price includes television rights and the real estate that Fenway Park is built on, and it is clearly worth significantly more. But it also seems clear that by buying the Expos, holding on to them for a few years, and then reselling, the other twenty-nine owners stood to make a significant amount of money. The purchase price for franchise rights for the Diamondbacks and Devil Rays in 1995 was $130 million each, so a well-established and now competitive team should have sold for significantly more money than the owners paid. It was also helpful that the person who sold the Expos was able to buy another team in the league, with a loan from the league, so that he could share in the pot. He didn't have to find a legitimate owner or even try to make a profit on the sale. The profit would come via the shared revenue that MLB would dole out.

Should an owner who failed so miserably in one city get a chance to run another franchise? The ease with which this owner was able to abandon one failing franchise to acquire a better one sent a signal to fans in South Florida: team owners aren't interested in the community; they are only interested in the money. Though it looks like he didn't make much money on the deal, what will his share of the profits be when MLB resells the franchise to a city dying for a team? In a day when free agency is squeezing profit margins, owners are finding other ways to line their pockets. Loria could end up being the hero in Miami and an enemy to the city of Montreal if the potential stadium deal goes through in South Florida. He will have accomplished something that two other owners have failed to do. Only time will tell how history judges him.

Though I was just over halfway through my tour now, the traveling was taking its toll. Had this been a good idea? On a layover on my way to St. Louis, I had a couple of chance meetings that demonstrated that I shouldn't limit my discussions to fans in the stadiums. There were opportunities to talk baseball all around me, and that's why this trip could never be a bad idea. I sat down next to a couple of young men, choosing my seat so that I could easily see the *Sportscenter* repeat from the night before. One of the guys noticed my interest as we watched a replay of Bonds going deep and asked off handedly about where most of his homers land—left, center, or right. My guess was that almost all go right, especially since the wind in Pac Bell blows in so sharply from left field. We moved on to a discussion about Tom Glavine and whether umps give him an advantage on ball and strike counts. I shared my opinion that he did get some help, but that he had earned it, much in the same way that Bonds had earned his small strike zone. Umps trust his eye at this point; if he doesn't swing, it isn't in the zone. By now, I suspected this guy might be more than a fan. When I had casually met coaches with the Giants, they had quizzed me to see if I really knew the players and the game in general. Ron Wotus, of the Giants, had asked my opinion of his team, and when I shared my quick supposition, he and the other coaches all looked knowingly at each other. They never let on whether they thought I was right or wrong. Had I proven myself, or was I just a mouthy no-nothing? In the airport, this guy's questions had a similar tone. They were too specific off the bat to have come from a casual fan. I asked him who he was and discovered that he was a young catcher in the Cubs system. He was on his way to AAA—Joe Girardi had gone on the Cubs DL, and the Iowa catcher had been called up. Though this fellow might never make it to "The Show," part of his job is to think about hitting and pitching on a much different level than those of us who merely watch from the stands.

This helps to explain the gulf that exists between players and fans. Halfway through my tour, I realized I wasn't just coming to understand why we love to watch baseball; I was learning to think about the game in different terms. It is only by understanding the "insider's" point of view that the fan's opinion begins to matter. The differences between the fan's perspective and the player's is what had caused the All-Star Game debacle to occur. From this point on, I was less concerned with MLB's efforts to appease the fans and more concerned about bridging this gulf. The doubt began to trickle away and was replaced by fervor. This project was important.

On the plane, as I was reading Peter Golenbeck's *The Spirit of St. Louis: A History of the St. Louis Cardinals and Browns*, an older couple sat down next to me. The woman asked if I was a baseball fan, and I explained that I was traveling around the leagues to find out what it felt like to be a fan at each stadium. When I asked her if she was a fan, she said, "Well, my uncle was a manager and he signed Jackie Robinson," in the sweetest Southern accent I could ever remember hearing.

"Your uncle was Branch Rickey?" I asked.

"You've heard of Uncle Branch?" she responded.

I turned the pages in my book and there was a picture of Rickey as a young man. I was blown away by the serendipity of it all. We sat and talked about her experiences growing up in southern Ohio and going to Reds game while her uncle was with the club. She and her husband had lived near many major-league clubs, and she told me stories of visiting several of the old stadiums, long since vacated, and of stopping at the Metrodome on game day just to get a foot-long hot dog.

Many of her memories of Branch Rickey were not tied to baseball, but the timing of the meeting really drove home how integral the sport is to many people's lives. Just hearing her speak about arguably the most influential man in modern baseball gave me chills. That's easily as powerful as McGwire's home run.

Busch Stadium
San Francisco Giants @ St. Louis Cardinals
July 17, 2002
Section 232, Row 6, Seat 9

The St. Louis Cardinals were playing a series against the Giants, in front of the touted "best fans in baseball," and I felt I was about to see something special. The stadium, a round multipurpose arena just like the ones in Philly and Cincinnati, reminded me of the encircled baseball pit of Riverfront, a fond memory from my youth. Here, though, the tops of the buildings and the St. Louis Arch peeked in from above to check in on the game. In one clever architectural detail, the arches that hold up the overhang in the upper deck mirror the larger arch outside. Though I had seen them a thousand times on television, this detail now seemed to give the "cookie-cutter" stadium a connection to the city outside.

The game was a big draw, since it was the only time the Giants, and specifically Bonds, would be in town, but I immediately got the sense that these fans came as often as they could no matter who the visitors were. Everywhere one looked there was a sea of red shirts, most bearing the names of the players on the field. I expected to see a strong following for McGwire, and I was slightly surprised to see that jerseys people were wearing provided a reminder of the franchise's entire history: the slugger Stan Musial, the great pitcher Bob Gibson, "The Wizard" Ozzie Smith, and the present-day stars, Edmonds, Drew, Vina, and Pujols. I thought I knew right away why St. Louis is considered baseball's best town: their history includes many championships and a host of stars that brought national attention to the city.

St. Louis was one of the original towns to host a franchise in both leagues, and it represented the far westernmost and southernmost frontier of the game until 1958. Originally an amateur club, the Browns became a professional nine after local boosters, embarrassed by the local amateur team's poor performance, raised $20,000 to field a team in the National Association. The first general manager hired players away from Brooklyn and Philadelphia. The team finished fourth in 1875. They joined the National League upon its founding in 1876 but only lasted two years. Their president, J-B. C. Lucas, took over as manager in the second year and did horribly, signing four dubious players away from Louisville to strengthen the team. It was revealed midway through the season that the four had taken money to throw games while with their previous team and that Lucas knew it. The four were barred for life, Lucas resigned as president, and the team withdrew from the National League.

The team played the next few years against other independent semi-pro teams, and in 1881 they were purchased by Chris Von Der Ahe, a local beer baron. The National League, run by Al Spalding, had strict rules about the sale of alcohol and gambling on the premises. Prior to the 1881 season, Spalding had kicked four franchises out of the league, two for selling alcohol. Two of those teams, along with the Browns and several other independent team owners, founded the American Association. The Brown Stockings, as they were then called, had great success, winning the American Association championship each year from 1885 to 1888. In 1884, Henry Lucas, the brother of J-B. C. Lucas, wanted to start a National League franchise. He was refused the right to do so and decided to form a new league to compete against the National League. His idea was to create a league that would revolutionize the way baseball owners treated their players, and the Union Association was formed. He paid higher salaries and left disciplinary matters up to the players. The local franchise, the St. Louis Maroons, was quite successful, with a 94-19 record. Before the end of the season, however, many teams had dropped out of the league. Lucas, though, had managed to impress, if not frighten, the leaders of the National Association, and they offered him a franchise on the condition that he disband the UA. The Maroons were not very effective after joining the National League, and in 1885, as the cross-town Browns began a streak of success, disaster struck. The Maroons' park burned down due to a fireworks display gone awry, injuring several spectators in the process. Lucas was liable, and since the Browns were winning the hearts (and dollars) of St. Louis, he had no means to regain his lost fortune. The team was sold to William T. Brush and moved to Indianapolis.

In 1891, after much wrangling by unhappy players and the team's frequent jumping from league to league, Van der Ahe worked out a deal for the Browns and the three other American Association teams to switch to the National League. Once there, the Browns had little success. By 1887, the team would finish twenty-two games behind eleventh-place Louisville. After Von der Ahe became embroiled in legal trouble, the other owners revoked his right to own a National League franchise in 1899. The team was sold to the Robison brothers, and players with talent, including Denton "Cy" Young, were shipped off to Cleveland. The uniforms were redesigned as part of a plan to change the team's image, and the socks were changed from brown to bright red. A newspaperman by the name of Willie Hall is credited with dubbing them the Cardinals.

In 1902, with the founding of the American League, a Milwaukee franchise was awarded to a Cincinnati businessman named Robert Lee Hedges. Hedges immediately moved the team to St. Louis and changed its name to the Browns. The American League had been founded to compete with the National League, with the new league's major distinction being that it would allow Sunday games and permit the sale of beer in the ballpark. These Browns never had much success. They finished in the bottom three of the league thirty-four times in fifty-three years and first only once, in 1944, in the middle of World War II. In 1951, Bill Veeck, former owner of the Cleveland Indians, purchased the team. He would own them for only a few years, but during that time he would become famous for several publicity stunts, including sending Eddie Gaedel, a midget, up to bat. In 1954, the Browns were sold to a Baltimore businessman, the team was moved, and they began play as the Orioles.

The Cardinals also had several unsuccessful years, until 1911, when ownership passed to one of Robison's daughters, who hired Miller Huggins to come in and run the team. In 1914, they finished in third place, and the team was sold again, this time to several businessmen, including Sam Breadon. Breadon recognized the need to hire a real baseball man and brought in a young Branch Rickey to be the vice president and general manager. Rickey created the farm system as we know it today as a means to stock up on young talent and to hide players from other organizations while their skills improved. Rogers Hornsby soon became one of the great stars of St. Louis and led the Cards, as player/manager, to their first World Series victory against the Yankees in 1926. Thirty-nine-year-old Grover Cleveland Alexander pitched the second and the sixth games for the Redbirds, winning both games, and came on to save the seventh, much like Randy Johnson did in 2001 for the Arizona Diamondbacks. The team met the Yankees again in 1928, but lost. By 1934, they had been to the championship series three more times, winning twice.

The Cardinals of the 1930s, dubbed the "Gas House Gang," included Dizzy and Daffy Dean, Joe Medwick, Leo Durocher, Pepper Martin, and Johnny Mize, all of whom were inducted into the Baseball Hall of Fame. With the additions of Stan Musial and Enos Slaughter, the 1940s were much like the 1930s for the Cards, including four pennants and three World Series championships between 1942 and 1946. Stan Musial went on to win seven batting titles and three MVP awards.

The Cardinals were sold in 1953 to August A. Busch Jr. in an effort to thwart a purchase that would have resulted in a move to another city. During Busch's forty-two years of ownership, the team got a new stadium in 1967 and saw its way to three World Series Championships in five appearances. Three of those Series came in five years in the 1960s, as Bob Gibson set NL pitching records and Lou Brock stole fifty bases a season for nine seasons. These weren't the only players to win accolades. Ken Boyer and Joe Torre both won NL MVP awards, Torre's coming in 1971. The 1970s also witnessed Lou Brock breaking the record for career-stolen bases set by Ty Cobb. The 1980s brought three more trips to the World Series, with one victory in 1982, and an All-Star shortstop in Ozzie Smith, who would win the Gold Glove thirteen times. When new owners took over in 1996, Tony LaRussa was hired as manager, and soon after, Mark McGwire was acquired from Oakland.

The history of the Cardinals franchise rests on the successes and stars of its past and present, and they belong in the same echelon as the Yankees in either category. Though they have gone decades here and there without winning seasons, they always have had a hero to carry them through the bleak periods. When I stood in the stands, I could see many generations of fans, all of whom could tell you a story or two about a great player they had seen as a kid, often comparing him to a current redbird. Baseball in St. Louis is intertwined with the milestones of each of its citizens.

As the game began, I settled into my seat in front of three men from Illinois. One was a Cards fan, another was a Cubs fan, and the third was a White Sox fan who had brought his six-year-old son. The Cubs fan was rooting for the Giants, the White Sox fan was rooting for a good game, and of course the third fellow wanted the Redbirds to win. It was a lot of fun, until the little guy, after consuming ice cream and lemonade, discovered that the two substances don't mix in a young child's tummy and threw up on his dad. Needless to say, they headed home. The people around me were all chatting happily as the game got underway. Though the chatting continued, everyone was paying very close attention, when a man got to second base, the conversation ceased. They might have wanted to hear about how their companion's job was going, but once a runner got into scoring position, baseball became priority number one, whether it was the first inning or the sixth. Unlike the Braves fans I had seen, nothing took their attention away from what was happening on the field. Here, getting a hit is exciting, but getting a hit with a man on is something to really cheer about. In St. Louis, the interest lies with the game rather than the players, and they know the game very well, with even the least interested person in the park able to spot the hit-and-run.

I had already stopped seeing baseball as an uncontrolled series of events that led from the first pitch to either victory or loss, realizing the game is composed of a very well ordered series of "plays." If you really know baseball, there is little guessing about what should happen next. The key is to have players who can execute, which both the Cardinals and the Giants had in 2002, and to have a guy in charge that knows the pattern. Some might say this isn't a particularly romantic way to experience the game, but understanding it on this level, caring about it as much, and sharing that experience might be what makes baseball so special. Its seeming simplicity, despite its actual complexity, could be the difference between baseball and other sports. The Cardinals fans as a whole understand this in a way that no other teams' fans do.

In the end, the two teams split the pair of games. Both would eventually meet again in the playoffs, with the Giants winning the NLCS and proceeding on to the World Series.

Kauffman Stadium
Cleveland Indians @ Kansas City Royals
July 19, 2002
Section 50, Row V, Seat 5

The Kansas City experience was the opposite in every way from the one in St. Louis despite being just across the state. I arrived at the ballpark, which sits outside of town just off the interstate, far from any apparent civilization, and found very few people waiting outside.

I suspected that the Indians wouldn't be a very big draw in Kansas City. The weather was humid but not nearly as bad as it had been in St. Louis. I couldn't imagine what the park looked like inside, but from the interstate, I could see the seating within the beautiful bowl. I met a father and his son who were moving from Ohio to Denver. They had been driving the moving van when they saw the stadium from the interstate and decided to call mom to tell her they would be arriving late tomorrow. They were stopping to see a game.

After purchasing a great seat and making my way inside, I discovered what appeared to be a brand new park. The seats had been replaced a couple of years earlier, and the entire stadium seemed immaculate. If it weren't for the dated design of the Royals' logo and crown motif, I would have thought this was a brand new park. The location, though it seemed a peculiar choice, contributed to the building's simple character. Named for the original owners of the Royals, Kauffman Stadium harkened back to the days when baseball was played in cornfields. It's as close as one comes to a "Field of Dreams" in major-league ball—it seemed as if someone had built the park and simply waited for folks to show up. It was comfortable, the people were friendly, and the seats were close to the action.

There were few people milling around to see batting practice, yet they seemed to be from out of town. By the time the game started, though, more than 20,000 fans had entered the building, including many people from Illinois and Iowa who had come down for the game. I met a few older men who had come out to see their friend throw out the first pitch. They wore old Royals hats and talked glowingly of past heroes George Brett and Bo Jackson. They said they came to games only rarely these days, since the tickets were expensive and the team on the field wasn't that good. Instead, they preferred to go up to Des Moines to see the Iowa Cubs play. The baseball, they explained, was just as good as what they could expect to see here, and the tickets were more reasonable. They weren't the only people who mentioned this, so it shouldn't be a surprise to learn that the Triple-A Iowa Cubs set attendance records in 2002. For their part, the Royals seemed to be playing Triple-A ball at the major-league level. The people here claimed to be loyal Royal fans, but as they talked, it seemed that their allegiance was a matter of habit rather than genuine inspiration. Following the Royals is simply what one does in these parts, I supposed.

It hasn't always been this way in Kansas City. Early on, the Kansas City Monarchs made their mark as one of the more successful and popular teams of the Negro League. Later, the city managed to lure away the struggling Philadelphia Athletics from the East. The A's didn't stay more than a few years, but in 1969 Major League Baseball expanded and baseball returned to Kansas City following Ewing Kaufman and his wife Muriel's purchase of a new franchise.

The Royals moved into their present-day home in 1973 and quickly began reaping the benefits of their farm system, which included George Brett and Frank White. The team became a powerhouse, winning its division each year from 1976 to 1978 and making its first World Series appearance in 1980 against the Philadelphia Phillies. They didn't win that year, but they returned to the Fall Classic in 1985, beating the rival St. Louis Cardinals in seven games. Besides Brett, the Royals had Amos Otis, Freddie Patek, Frank White, and Bret Saberhagen, a core talented enough to win over more than a few fans.

In 2000, the Royals were sold to David Glass, former president and CEO of Wal-Mart. Having served as both the executive vice president of finance and the chief financial advisor of the largest retailer in the world, Glass pays close attention to the Royals' bottom line, insisting that the team turn a profit each year. The Royals entered the 2003 season having cut their payroll (which was already one of the lowest in baseball) in an effort to balance the books. Although many owners see their franchises as long-term investments, preparing for losses in the short term, Glass seems to expect to turn a profit each season. As a result, the Royals may suffer. The problem is not new: August Busch also expected to turn a profit in his early years owning the Cardinals, and the team suffered for it.

While in KC, I noticed a lack of "buzz" about the franchise. There was your standard advertising around the town, but I saw little to accentuate the positives of this team, which are many, reminding folks why they should embrace baseball again. There was little in-game promotion of the players, nothing to make those in the stands think of the team as a "family." Unfortunately, because of the team's budget issues, the players seem to be either castoffs from bigger market teams or perennial trade-bait—either way, they are not very marketable to fans.

Kansas City desperately needs a franchise player to build their team around, and to capture the fans imagination.

Even though the Kansas City Monarchs, a Negro League team, set the stage for future major-league teams in the city, an African-American fan base never really developed here. Though more than a third of the population of Kansas City is African-American, I saw very few black people in the stands during my visit. Though the Negro Leagues Museum is located in Kansas City and the Royals include former Monarch Buck O'Neil as part of their history, the franchise doesn't seem to have much appeal within KC's African-American community. This might be due to the fact that there hasn't been an identifiable black star on the team since Bo Jackson.

I had arrived during a seven-game winning streak by the Royals. I saw wins eight and nine, and listened as they went for ten as I drove back to St. Louis to catch my plane. Attendance picked up for win number eight, and there was a definite buzz in the stands for win number nine. The team that the Indians now fielded was very different from the team that I had watched in the early weeks of June. With the trade of Colon to Montreal and injury to Jim Thome, the Indians were a much younger and inexperienced team that day. The Royals won the first game 8 to 5, but they allowed four solo home runs. The Indians' pitchers, though, combined to walk five and hit one batter. The only homer they allowed was a grand slam by Raul Ibanez. The second game, a daytime affair under a blazing sun, was a bit better from a pitching standpoint, with Roberto Hernandez facing off against Jaret Wright. The Royals won the game 7-5, cutting short a Cleveland rally in the ninth that included a two-run homer by Chris Magruder.

The Royals staff was wonderful and friendly. The setting was beautiful, and the match-up was fairly even. In my two days there I received a Royals travel mug and a powder blue Kansas City t-shirt, both of which were of surprisingly high quality for promotional giveaways. If the quality of the baseball had been better, this could have easily ranked as my most comfortable and enjoyable baseball experience in the major leagues. But considering the lack of excited fans in the stands and identifiable stars on the field, I think I too would go see the Iowa Cubs next time.

Veterans Stadium
San Francisco Giants @ Philadelphia Phillies
July 31, 2002
Section 520, Row 2, Seat 6

My next stop was in Philadelphia, for a midweek series against the Giants. I had originally planned to see the Phillies later in the year, but with the threat of a strike looming, I needed to rearrange my plans. This meant I would once again see the Giants play. I had already seen the Phillies several times on the road this year, at Shea and then twice in Detroit.

The Giants' outfield had been ravaged by injury, and though the team had been early contenders, the situation now looked grim. Two days earlier, the Giants had traded for Kenny Lofton; maybe this would keep hope alive while the team waited for Shinjo and Marvin Bernard to heal.

Most National League players with whom I had spoken had named Philadelphia as the city with the most hostile fans, and so I was eager to experience Veterans Memorial Stadium. Several years prior, a football fan was thrown from the upper deck of the Vet to his death because he was rooting for the "wrong" team, an incident that corroborated the rumors that I had heard. At the time, the media also expressed their concern about the fans. Though everyone acknowledged that New York and Boston were tough places to play, Vet fans were "the worst."

The history of baseball in Philadelphia began with the formation of the Phillies in 1883. The early Phillies had great success. They featured three Hall of Fame outfielders, Ed Delahanty, Billy Hamilton, and Sam Thompson, all of whom hit over .400 in 1894. Delahanty hit over .400 three times, winning a batting title in 1899 with a .410 average. When the American League was formed, many National League stars were signed away, including Delahanty and Phillies second baseman Nap Lajoie. Both men went on to win batting titles for the American League, Delahanty with the newly formed Philadelphia Athletics. The loss of the two stars had an immediate impact on the early Phillies, and the team plummeted in the standings. It wasn't until 1915 that the Phillies would get to a World Series. That year, Grover Cleveland Alexander won thirty-one games while pitching four one-hitters, and Gavvy Cravath set the home-run record, with twenty-four, a record that would stand until Babe Ruth broke it four years later. The Phillies lost that Series, however, in five games.

Though the Phillies acquired some great players in the late 1920s and early 1930s, including Chuck Klein and Lefty O'Doul, they failed to contend. By

1942, the club had lost more than one hundred games for five straight seasons. By the end of the 1940s, more great players had begun to arrive, including Robin Roberts, Richie Ashburn, and Dick Sisler. In 1949, the so-called Whiz Kids finished third in the National League, the Phillies highest finish since 1917, and then won the pennant in 1950 by one game (nearly blowing a seven-game lead, which they enjoyed with eleven games left to play in the season). They lost the World Series to the Yankees in four games.

The 1960s would play out similar to previous decades, with great stars abounding on their roster but little on-field success. In 1964, Richie Allen was crowned Rookie of the Year and Jim Bunning pitched a perfect game against the Mets. They suffered a terrible end to their season, though, going 2-10 in their final 12 and blowing a six and a half game division lead. The collapse shocked their fans. Still, 12,000 were waiting at the airport to greet the team when they returned following the final game.

The 1970s brought new stars, such as Mike Schmidt and Steve Carlton, and the team enjoyed numerous successes culminating in a World Series win in 1980, their first ever. This marked the end of the longest World Series drought in history until that point. The Phillies returned to the October Classic just three years later but lost to Baltimore in five games, and they returned again in 1993, losing to the Blue Jays. This was the only year in the 1990s when the Phillies managed to finish with a winning record, though they did see several of their former stars inducted into the Baseball Hall of Fame.

I arrived at Veterans Stadium shortly after Scott Rolen was dealt to the Cardinals in a five-player deal. He was slated to become the biggest free agent on the market and had turned down a lucrative offer by the Phillies, citing a desire for more money and a feeling that Philly ownership wasn't interested in winning. A trade involving Rolen had been speculated throughout the season, so it was likely a relief for the team when it was finalized. Over the past two years, Philadelphia had traded away some big stars, most notably Curt Schilling, in an effort to cut costs. This season, the Phillies had gotten off to a terrible start, but they had managed to get to around .500 by late July.

It was a midweek series, but the crowd at the game still seemed small considering that this would be the only visit by Bonds and the Giants. Waiting outside the stadium, I met a family of Mets fans in the parking lot who had come to see Bonds play. There was a rumor swirling around, however (originating from a local sports radio network), that Bonds was not going to take the field that evening. The few people who had come early were filled with disappointment; some even contemplated not staying for the game. In the end, Bonds was in right field, and over the course of the evening he managed to get two doubles (one a ground-rule), a home run, a strike out, and an intentional walk in the ninth with two men on base. His performance justified the hype, even though the Giants lost 8-6.

Even from the outside, the Vet felt desolate and cold. Once I entered, I felt the atmosphere warm up a little, but I still felt far from the action. The tasteful blue seats cooled the mood for me, and at this game I could see a lot of empty ones. In the stadium's concourse, I found a wealth of baseball-related information and activities, including one of my favorites, the opportunity to hold different sized bats used by players around the league. These included a short piece of wood like the one Bonds uses as well as replicas of the lumber used by Alex Rodriguez, Vladimir Guerrero, and the new local hero, Pat Burrell.

Those who attended to watch batting practice were loyal old-time fans. They had been watching the Phillies forever, and their heroes included Richie Ashburn, Richie Allen, and others. I also met a few young fans who really liked Matt Franco. Even though he was only a part-time player, they thought he was a hustler who came up with key hits. A couple of older gentlemen sitting along the first-base side shared some memories. One told me that he enjoyed coming to the game so much, that he would come straight from work two hours away, see batting practice, watch the game, then drive home arriving in time to go back to his third-shift job. The Phillies were weak at the time, so he couldn't count on them to win, but he loved baseball so much that he continued to come. He could recall what it was like in the past, when the Phillies were winners, and that was enough to preserve his loyalty and keep him coming to see a less-than-stellar team take the field. He was disgusted by all the discussion of a strike, but he felt he would continue to come regardless of the outcome of the labor dispute. His friend said he would never come again, no matter what, if the players went on strike this time. He actually hoped that the players would be foolish enough to strike, "so those millionaires will learn a lesson." He liked baseball, but he couldn't believe the players were still whining about money. In the past, we wanted the players to win the labor disputes, but now players are hard to identify with. It's hard to root for an underdog when you can't figure out who the underdog is. Here was a union man wanting the players union to knuckle under.

In the outfield, I met an African-American usher named Tony who was probably among the biggest Phillies fans in the stadium. He told me about how he had come to the games in his twenties to see Jackie Robinson play. The stadium wasn't segregated by law at the time, but generally black fans sat together in certain sections. When the Dodgers came to town, about a third of those in the stands were black. Tony and his friends were serious Phillies fans, but when Jackie Robinson took the field, they couldn't help but root for the Dodgers. Philadelphia was the last National League team to integrate, and the white fans here were particularly rough on Robinson. Watching Robinson persevere while the locals taunted him surely couldn't have been easy for the African-Americans sitting in the stands. Though Tony loved his Phillies and hoped for their success, Robinson's struggle was also important to him. "I kept pretty quiet during those games," he said.

In the Vet, the bullpen is open and is situated just under a section of seats, so relievers often have to deal with fans throwing things into the pen. Many of the fans here were tough-looking men who weren't shy about demonstrating their feelings for the team; the Phillies' recent lack of success seemed to have little effect on these individuals. There weren't many families there despite the opportunity to see one of the game's greatest active players. The fans sitting around me, mostly men in their forties and fifties, were very familiar with their team—and very bitter over its recent managerial decisions. One man shouted, "Make us forget about the trade," each time a player who came over in the recent Scott Rolen deal or the Curt Schilling trade with Arizona a few years earlier came to bat. This man seemed to know his team's history, and even though the Phillies were winning he was still so frustrated by the personnel choices that he didn't seem to enjoy it. One fan mentioned that he didn't blame Rolen for wanting to leave, while another said that he felt he should have settled for the offer so the team could have someone to build around.

During the game, I heard little cheering and a lot of cynicism. In fact, the fans seemed so angry that I couldn't understand why they had come. The ones I talked to told me that they loved their Phillies. After their collapse in the 1964 season, more than one million fans came through their turnstiles the following year, demonstrating the resiliency and loyalty of the Philly fan, which still exists today. Philadelphia, like St. Louis, had managed to put great players on the field even through their bleak periods. Unfortunately, those bleak periods always ran longer in Philly.

With Philadelphia's proximity to other cities with pro teams, the few local stars had failed to garner much National attention. Local baseball rooters also had choices of other teams to watch, some having great success while Philadelphia remained in the cellar. They also had teams close by to compare their Phillies to. Due to the team's failure to measure up, frustration has become the dominant feeling at the ballpark. Perhaps this is the reason why the fans at this game were so tough—these were the ones who were able to stick it out and stay loyal.

In the off-season of 2002, though, Philadelphia made some moves indicating that they were ready to win. The 2003 season was their last at the Vet, and the team wanted to move into their new stadium with a contender. They signed Jim Thome away from Cleveland and David Bell from San Francisco and traded with Atlanta for Kevin Millwood in hopes that would help bring a winner to their new home. This new commitment to success has paid off, and Citizens Bank Park is quite full for most games. It's a wonderful place to watch a game, a vast improvement over the Vet. Another season of disappointment, however, may dampen the newfound enthusiasm and optimism of the Philly fan.

Comiskey Stadium
Seattle Mariners @ Chicago White Sox
August 8, 2002,
Box 137, Row 23, Seat 6

My experience with White Sox fans, my first team to see in August, was surprisingly similar to the one I had in Philadelphia. I saw the White Sox play both the Anaheim Angels and the Seattle Mariners, two very strong teams, and though the White Sox played well, it was clear on both days that the home team was outmatched.

In my research, I had seen a number of photos of the quaint and boxy Old Comiskey Stadium. I had also heard the stories of everything they had gotten wrong at the New Comiskey Stadium, since renamed U.S. Cellular Field. Yet I was still unprepared for how antiseptic the park would feel when I entered.

The stadium was shiny and clean, but it lacked the character of the old parks (and even of the new ones that had recreated an old-time feel). I imagine that this was the feeling people got when they entered the cookie cutter-stadiums of the 1960s and early 1970s for the first time. The amenities were great, but the building felt more like a hospital than a sporting arena, and the ushers and vendors were the rudest I had ever encountered. The in-game entertainment was repetitive, with several incarnations of the "race game" used in other stadiums. The organ music was quaint, but some of the prerecorded selections, such as Ricky Martin's "Livin' La Vida Loca," seemed peculiar.

Fans all around the park were pining for the "Old Comiskey," and each one in turn pointed at the upper deck and explained that they refused to sit "up there." I had heard it was pretty steep, so I wasn't too surprised. I headed to my seat, but the escalators were out of service. Once I ascended the ramp to the upper deck, I was shocked that a building inspector had approved such a steep incline for a seating area. I was also surprised that no one had ever fallen.

My seat was in the front row, so I wasn't too concerned for my safety at first. After I sat down, however, I discovered that the edge of the balcony cut off the view of the entire first-base side, all the way to the pitcher's mound. I would have to lean forward, very far forward, to be able to see the batter and the base runner. I moved into an empty seat two rows up, but when I did, I was overcome by vertigo. The rows were very narrow. When trying to climb over people's feet, I felt as though I would lose my balance and fall forward over the balcony onto the seats below. There would have been plenty of walking room if the row had been empty, but with people sitting there it was nearly impossible to get by. One woman sitting in front of me commented on how much ketchup fans had spilled on her as they tried to navigate the row behind her. It took about six innings before I no longer felt I was rolling forward into oblivion. The view from two rows back actually allowed me to see most of the field, but I had a hard time enjoying it.

The fans I met upstairs were all of the fair-weather variety, which may explain why they were willing to sit upstairs. Mostly they were visitors from out of town, just catching a game in Chicago while they were there. Tickets are easy to come by on the South Side of Chicago, and so they decided to check out a game. Downstairs is where the real White Sox regulars sit.

If I had to say two things about Chicago fans, it's that they love their baseball, and they love their beer. Joe Balitewicz, a local fan, reminded me that announcer Harry Caray had called the Old Comiskey "the world's largest outdoor saloon." I'd say not much has changed, despite Caray's departure from the South Side. The fans I spoke with are proud of the connection between beer and baseball, which is no more apparent than in Chicago (sorry Brewers fans). I was reminded that many of the Midwestern teams were founded, or at some point owned, by local brewers who wanted a marketplace for their product.

The Sox fans I met also felt that they were the "real" baseball fans in Chicago. Their roots were in the working class (more so than their cross-town rivals), and baseball seemed to mean more to them than it did to Cubs fans. On the train ride home I met some college students who had attended the game. They had grown up on the North Side but were White Sox fans nevertheless, thinking it was too "establishment" to be a Cubs fan.

The White Sox were one of the original members of the American League, which owner Charles Comiskey was instrumental in bringing together. He purchased the St. Paul Saints of the Western League, a junior pro organization spread across the Western states, and moved them to Chicago in 1900. They won the pennant that year and the next. In 1906 they went to the World Series—the only all-Chicago final—and won it four games to two.

Old Comiskey Park was built in 1910. In 1917, the Sox returned to the World Series and beat the New York Giants. Two years later, they were back again but lost to the Reds. More notably, they become caught up in the "Black Sox" scandal, where eight players were accused of throwing the World Series. Although no court of law ever found them guilty, the scandal had scarred the game deeply, and the newly appointed commissioner banned all of them from the majors for life. Because of this, gambling was looked upon as the worst infraction anyone involved with baseball could commit.

Though the White Sox would feature many great players through the 1930s and 1940s, it wasn't until 1951 that they would pass the one million mark in attendance. At the end of that decade they would return to the World Series, losing to the Dodgers in six games. The team would have a number of different owners before returning to the Series, including Bill Veeck, who bought the team in 1958, sold it three years later, and repurchased it again in 1975.

Veeck's promotional ideas garnered much criticism, but he managed to draw crowds in Chicago just as he had in St. Louis in the 1950s and Cleveland in the 1940s. Veeck is responsible for both putting on fireworks nights and placing names on the backs of uniforms. He also made one other important contribution to baseball. He discovered a tax loophole that allowed him to deduct the cost of players from the purchase price of a team (much as factory owners would write off the cost of machinery). Now, over the course of the first seven years of ownership, owners can depreciate the value of their players. This allows owners to declare a net profit much smaller than it actually is.

Veeck's repurchase of the team in 1975 marked the beginning of a new era of baseball on the South Side. Two years later, the "Hitmen," as they were dubbed, won ninety games. Veeck again sold the team in 1981 to its present ownership group, headed by Jerry Reinsdorf. They made it back to the post-season in 1983 but lost to the Orioles in the ALCS. Ten years later they would suffer the same fate at the hands of the Blue Jays.

In 2000, the Sox produced a season that would draw many South Side fans back to the park, winning ninety-five games and capturing the Central Division title. Though they lost in the Division Series, their competitiveness inspired hope in many local fans. That magical season, and the brief appearance in the post-season, seems to have sustained their audience since. While the 2000 team continued to age and was not able to return to form, many White Sox fans, who had generally been absent since the strike of 1994, told me that the resurgence of their club had restored their love of baseball. In 2003, they looked like contenders once again, but in the end they finished four games behind Minnesota.

Miller Park
Montreal Expos @ Milwaukee Brewers
August 10, 2002,
Section 122, Row 17, Seat 4

I have to admit it. At this point in the summer, I was getting pretty tired. It was the second week of August, I had only seven teams to go, and talk of a possible strike was heating up. Today I was going to watch the Milwaukee Brewers play the Montreal Expos. Not only were they the two last-place teams in their respective divisions, but also the Expos weren't even sure if they would exist the following year. After watching two good games in Chicago, it was somewhat difficult to get into the experience, but nevertheless here I was, searching out true Brewers fans.

The Brewers' history is short but not without some highlights. After the Braves left Milwaukee for Atlanta in 1966, they left a void for many Wisconsinites. Bud Selig, along with a coalition of businessmen, set out to bring Major League baseball back to Milwaukee. They lobbied the Chicago White Sox to play several games in Milwaukee's County Stadium in 1968. When baseball expanded for the 1969 season, everyone was sure that the National League would choose Milwaukee. Instead, Montreal and San Diego got the nod, while the American League chose Kansas City and Seattle. The Seattle team did so poorly (drawing only 677,000 for the entire season) that the owners considered turning the bankrupt team back over to the American League. Selig and his contingent wasted no time in purchasing the team and moving it to Milwaukee for the 1970 season.

The team played for thirty years at County Stadium. During that time, quite a few standout players wore the Brewers' uniform, including Hank Aaron for the final two years of his career. With the debut of Robin Yount in 1974 and the addition of Paul Molitor four years later, the club began its rise to the status of contender. During the 1981 off-season, key trades brought in Rollie Fingers, Pete Vuckovich, and Ted Simmons, and the Brewers made their first post-season appearance that year. In 1982, they made their first World Series appearance, losing to the St. Louis Cardinals in seven games. The following year, the club set its attendance record at 2,397,131. Robin Yount became their franchise player, playing twenty seasons with the Brewers and entering the Hall of Fame in 1999.

In 1995, Bud Selig, in consort with Governor Tommy Thompson, proposed a financing package that would see the Brewers get a publicly funded new stadium. The Brewers played their first game at Miller Park six years later, and that year they set a new Milwaukee attendance record at 2.8 million. In 1992, Selig resigned as team president to become the interim commissioner, and then later the commissioner, of Major League Baseball. The daily operations fell to his daughter, who resigned following the 2002 season.

The park is so beautiful that in the beginning it drew crowds on that quality alone. Before the games, the parking lot is filled with the scent of grilling meats from the numerous tailgaters, an integral part of the baseball experience in Milwaukee. The parking lot is set away from the stadium to accommodate fan activities, but no one seems to mind, since there is always plenty of parking.

Though the fans here seemed to enjoy the routine of coming to the park, I saw little enthusiasm for the game itself (although I suspect this had something to do with the quality of their opposition that series). The Brewers' lack of success over the years has created unparalleled apathy among the fans. There were many folks here who were fans of other teams, but simply came to the stadium because it was convenient to their present locale. The majority of those I spoke to didn't really care about the Brewers; going to a game was simply something to do. The fans had little to hold on to from their glory years—even Robin Yount, was employed by another club now (as a coach for the Arizona Diamondbacks). As in Kansas City, the comfort of the park and the friendliness of the ushers didn't make up for the dismal play on the field or the lack of hope in the hearts of the fans.

The love of the new park eventually wore off and attendance dropped after that first season. In 2004, however, things seemed to improve: the team played their best ball in years, finishing around .500, and attendance rose by one million. Perhaps with new stewards steering the ship, Milwaukee will one day have something to cheer about again, both on and off the field.

Wrigley Field
Houston Astros @ Chicago Cubs
August 12, 2002,
Aisle 229, Row 8, Seat 5

I returned to Chicago from my weekend in Milwaukee to see the Cubs play the Astros at Wrigley Field. Chicago's National League team began in 1876 as the White Stockings, with the formation of the Senior Major League. The term "Cubs" was coined in 1902, when a local paper noted the emerging young talent on the squad. The name stuck and was officially adopted in 1907. That early team went on to win four National League pennants and two World Series, in 1907 and 1908.

In 1926, the ten-year-old home of the Cubs was renamed Wrigley Field, after the owner of the team. Four years later, Hack Wilson homered 56 times and drove in a record 191 runs, a mark that still stands. The Cubs had many strong seasons after this point, appearing in four more World Series, including their last, in 1945, where they lost to Detroit in seven games. They wouldn't appear in the post season again until 1984. The Wrigley family sold the Cubs to the Tribune Company in 1981. Despite post-season berths in 1989, 1998, and 2003, the Cubs have not returned to the October classic. They now hold the record for the longest drought without a championship.

Cubs fans don't seem to mind, however. Fans come for the peaceful experience of watching baseball in MLB's quietest park, the second oldest in existence. The stadium is beautiful in a simple way, though the amenities are outdated and you may find yourself sitting behind a steel girder that completely obstructs your view of the field. As I mentioned, the stadium is quiet, and they still play mostly during the day (because of complaints about the giant lights from nearby residents). Wrigley was the last stadium to host night games. Lights were not even installed until 1988, and even then their use was restricted to eighteen games a season. That number was increased slightly over the years.

I had the privilege of seeing one of those rare night games, in which the Cubs would play the Astros. This was a particularly exciting game if you were a Houston fan. Kerry Wood was pitching against Roy Oswalt. With his team leading 1-0, Wood gave up back-to-back homers in the fourth to Jeff Bagwell and Daryle Ward, and the Astros never trailed again. Wood was ejected in the sixth inning for arguing balls and strikes with the umpire, and then Oswalt was ejected in the seventh for throwing at a batter. His reliever gave up a two-run home run to

Todd Hundley and then walked Bill Mueller. The next pitcher gave up another two-run shot to Sosa before getting the final out of the inning. Despite the rally, the Cubs lost 9-6.

The following afternoon's game was delayed by rain twice, prior to the first pitch and in the middle of the sixth inning. It seemed to me that a lot of the fans that day were men escaping work midday in time to see Sammy Sosa sprint to his place in right field. The stands were filled for both games, but the fans never got riled up for the Cubs. In fact, many folks seemed more interested in talking on their cell phones that afternoon, even though it was always a close game.

I wondered if the Cubs' World Series drought really mattered at all, since the fans seemed willing to fill the stands to watch a mediocre team. Wrigley provides such a relaxing, peaceful experience inside the lively Windy City that even when the team loses, people flock to the stadium in droves. With few distractions to draw their attention away from the field, fans are able to experience a simpler time, and the park is routinely filled with those who want to boast about playing hooky by running off to the park in the middle of the day. The escape that Wrigley provides is valuable, and it offers a great lesson to other organizations: loud and busy does not make a team successful at the box office. However, I must confess, I was a little disappointed that the team from the North Side didn't seem all that interested in winning games.

Thankfully, I was wrong. In 2003, the Cubs got off to an incredible start due to some off-season trades and some very talented homegrown pitchers. Maybe the Cubs don't need to win in order to be a "successful" franchise, but in 2003 they made it to the seventh game of the NLCS. Fans were seen weeping in the stands when they lost, and the cry of "wait until next year" wasn't the least bit comforting.

Metrodome
Baltimore Orioles @ Minnesota Twins
August 14, 2002,
Section 121, Row 25, Seat 14

The Minnesota Twins were the second team MLB was considering for contraction. The Twins franchise began as the Washington Senators with the formation of the American league in 1901. The team was purchased by the Griffith family 1912 and moved to Minnesota in 1960, taking on a new name that would honor both Minneapolis and St. Paul. In the 1962 season they climbed to second place in the standings led by a number of quality players, such as Tony Oliva, the first player to win consecutive batting titles in his first two seasons of play.

As the Senators, the organization had won a pennant in 1933, and now, just five years after becoming the Twins, they had won another, losing the World Series to Drysdale and Koufax's Dodgers. Despite losing the ALCS to Baltimore in both 1969 and 1970, the Twins managed to put together many fine seasons, led by several talented individuals including Rod Carew, Harmon Killebrew, and Bert Blyleven. In 1977, Carew led the league with a .388 average, 239 hits, 128 runs scored, and 100 RBI.

After playing twenty-one seasons at Metropolitan Stadium, the Twins moved into the Metrodome in 1982. The multipurpose stadium, which is also the home of the NFL's Minnesota Vikings, got the fans out of the cold, damp Minnesota weather, but it did little to provide a traditional baseball atmosphere. To make matters worse, the Griffith family signed a lease that included a minimum-attendance clause; if not met, it would allow Griffith to break the lease and move the club to Florida.

Fearing the loss of their team, local businessmen got together to buy blocks of tickets, but it wasn't until Carl Pohlad stepped forward to purchase the club that fans were sure it would remain in Minneapolis. The Twins won their first World Series in 1987, and the following year the team became the first in American League history to draw three million fans. The Twins won another Series in 1991, with the bat of Kirby Puckett and the pitching arm of Jack Morris beating Atlanta in seven games.

Pohlad began seeking funding for a new stadium in 1997. After failing to secure the necessary support, he entered into a tentative deal to sell the team to a North Carolina businessman who intended to move them. When the deal fell through, Pohlad signed a lease that would keep the Twins in the Metrodome through 2000.

In 2001, the Minnesota legislature again turned down a bill that would have provided public funds for a new stadium. Pohlad, disenchanted with being an owner of a small-market baseball team, now wanted out. With no apparent buyer on the horizon and no prospect of improving the team's status by building a new stadium, MLB chose the Twins as a possible second team to be contracted.

A gentleman outside the stadium before the game spoke with me about the many Wisconsin residents who cross the border to work and then return home to pay taxes rather than support the state where their jobs are. When Selig, the owner of the Wisconsin team that would most benefit from the Twins' removal, announced that the second team up for contraction would be the Twins, many Minnesotans saw this as MLB adding insult to injury.

Though they are badly in need of a new facility designed for baseball, the overall experience in the Metrodome isn't a bad one, mostly due to the warmth of the fans. The stadium is dank, and if you sit along the third-base line, you are looking into the lights the entire game. Between the lights and the noise created by the dome, extra-innings games, like the one I watched between the Twins and the Orioles, are not all that pleasant. The fans, however, were loyal and joyful as they cheered relentlessly for their team. Though the Twins had been slated for contraction, their play on the field had brought attention back to Minneapolis. They featured a number of young, emerging stars, including Torii Hunter and Jacque Jones, as well as a talented pitching staff. The baseball was exciting, and it was clear that this team wouldn't be going anywhere without a fight. The Twins really seem to be a member of the community, in much the same way the Cardinals are in St. Louis. Twenty-eight thousand people watched the Orioles prevail in fourteen innings during the first game, with Geronimo Gil hitting a solo home run to bring the score to 6-5. The Orioles won the next night as well, 3-1.

Throughout the Midwest, I had experienced what it meant to be part of the baseball family. Baseball seemed more ingrained in those towns, a lesson I had learned from individuals such as Branch Rickey's niece and the older men who had come of age watching baseball and drinking beer at Comiskey. Despite the discussion of a strike, these people seemed to look upon their local teams with pride, even if they were having tough seasons.

For Midwestern cities, getting a major-league team was a rite of passage, a sign that they'd made it. When the Braves moved to Milwaukee, newspapers of the time considered this a sign that it was a "big-league town."[16] Baseball helps to create a sense of community in the region, and this is perhaps the greatest gift the sport has given to many Americans. Most of these teams are now considered "small market" because of their low advertising revenues; however, it is their fans that baseball must take care to nurture. By filling the seats, they are the ones who will carry the game through its lean times—it's their respect for the game that provides the team with a place in their communities.

7

Connections and Community

I studied theater at a women's college in the Northeast. During my four years there, I met only a few other women who were very interested in professional baseball. Some came from families that casually followed the Mets or the Red Sox, but no one who crossed my path struck me as an avid fan. When I graduated in 1990, I went to work in New Haven, Connecticut. I ended up sharing an apartment with a few friends I had known while I was in school. After being surrounded primarily by women for four years, I now found myself living with four male roommates.

Though the guys I lived with were not serious organized sports fans, the masculine world I was now living in brought sports back to the forefront of my social world. I had never followed any sport other than baseball, so to make friends and find common ground with people I often played up my knowledge of the Reds, boasting about how well they would do in the upcoming season. Cincinnati started off strong that year, and the few hardcore baseball fans who wandered in and out of our apartment always teased me that the team would fall apart as the season progressed. I admitted that the team was too young to endure the long and grueling pennant race, but I wanted to believe they were going to hang in there.

After the hockey and basketball seasons came to a close, I was the only one in the house still following sports. I was invited to watch games at others' houses on Saturday afternoons, since many found it novel to have a female fan in the mix. Guys were surprised at how much I knew about the National League, and particularly my Reds. I learned a lot about baseball in general and the American League in particular that summer, since I was right in the middle of Red Sox and Yankee Country. As for the Reds, they did hang in there. They held first place wire to wire that year, and I followed every minute of it.

It was the first baseball season I had been completely immersed in since I was twelve years old. I even started collecting baseball cards again. I knew the entire team's stats, as well as their favored match-ups. I loved Paul O'Neill's feistiness and Chris Sabo's tenacity. When the playoffs came around, we had won the NL West, and the Pirates had won the East. Against Jim Leyland team's, which included Bonds, Bobby Bonilla, Andy Van Slyk, and Doug Drabeck, I didn't hold much hope for my young Reds—the team from the East simply had too much power.

Though my heart wasn't fully behind my team, I wagered with Pirate-fan friends on the outcome of the series—nothing much, $5, a six-pack, or something like that. When the Reds pulled off the victory the day after Drabeck pitched a gem to keep the Bucs alive, tears welled up in my eyes. The Reds were going to the World Series. They would be playing the Oakland A's, and again I didn't believe they would get even one victory. This would be the A's third appearance in the past three years. They were not only a fantastic team, but they also had experience on their side. I was invited to watch the games with friends whom I hadn't even known six months earlier. Throughout the Series, I regularly found myself in all-male dens rooting passionately for my team. Most of these guys knew the A's were going to win, but they appreciated my hopefulness and didn't root against me too loudly. They weren't A's fans per se, so the need to challenge my passion wasn't necessary. Also, since I was a girl, their usual male bravado wouldn't be required. After the Reds won the second game, I told Eric, one of the biggest sports enthusiasts in the room, that I thought they could win the whole thing. They just needed to win one in Oakland and they would gain the confidence to go all the way. Three nights later, after two victories in Oakland, the Reds had swept the A's and were the world champions.

The following summer, while I was still giddy from my team's victory, my boyfriend at the time, Jim, who was from New York, took me to my first baseball games in New York. We saw the Mets play the Reds (and the Reds won) and we saw the Yankees play his favorite team, the Milwaukee Brewers. (He had always liked Robin Yount.) This was back in the day when teams handed out small scorecards and pencils for free, and Jim gave me a refresher on how to keep score. (Why should we have to buy a program to get a scorecard these days?) We also ended up going to a game in Oakland later that summer, but all I remember about that trip is how cold California can be in August.

I moved back to Ohio after that summer, and the following year I took my nieces and nephews to games as often as I could convince them to go. My niece Rachael didn't care much about baseball. She had a difficult time following her first game: the Cardinals were playing the Reds, and their uniforms looked so similar from a distance that it was impossible to differentiate the base runner on first from the first baseman. That game in no way captured her imagination. Within two years, I met my future husband, a fellow who didn't care much for sports either, and we moved to Ithaca, New York, which is about as far away as one can get from baseball in the East. Again, without someone to talk about the game with, my interest in baseball waned. We married in 1995 and moved to New York City. My husband hated the city. He was from Ohio and longed to leave the urban life behind. It overwhelmed him. For my career though, New York was the next logical step, and I felt that his chosen profession in the food industry could certainly be pursued there as well. The relationship quickly deteriorated. We separated in the fall of 1997, and he returned to Ohio.

That winter was long and lonely, and I had little interest in anything but my job at Juilliard. I thought about going to baseball games when the season started in 1998, but I was still a little put off by the strike of 1995 and didn't really want to pay big-league prices to watch a game that didn't live up to my memories. Then, a group of colleagues bought a bunch of bleacher seats for a day game at Yankee Stadium (though few of them knew much about the Yankees). The only thing I knew was my hero from 1990, Paul O'Neill, was playing just in front of us, in right field. We cheered now and then, but mostly we drank beer and enjoyed the sunshine.

As 1998 went on, it became apparent that this was a special year. When the Reds came to town, I made a trip out to Shea on Friday night, just for nostalgia's sake. I went by myself, the first time I had ever done that, and the sights and smells opened the floodgates of my memory. As a kid I had never attended batting practice, but on this day I made a point to arrive in plenty of time. Unfortunately, due to the possibility of rain, BP was canceled. As I approached the edge of the seats, there was Ken Griffey, now the bench coach of the Reds, talking to Marty Brennaman, the announcer for the Reds since 1974. Again, my eyes welled up with tears of the joy at seeing the heroes of my childhood in the same place that I remember them—on the baseball field. The Reds won that night, and as I left I promised myself that I would come again to another game soon.

By June, there was a buzz that the home-run record was in jeopardy, though no one really thought it would be broken. McGwire and Sosa both were saying that if anyone could do it, it would be Ken Griffey Jr. Sosa then went on a tear, setting a record for homers hit in the month of June, with twenty. By August, I was watching the TV wherever I was for news of more home runs by either McGwire or Sosa. I wasn't rearranging my schedule around games yet, but if I happened to be in a bar or at the house of a friend with cable, I checked in to find out where it all stood. By early September, I began changing my plans in order to catch all the action. McGwire and Sosa had been so gracious and generous towards each other, despite the obvious toll that this drama was taking on them, that I couldn't help but root for them both. On September 8, as the ball sailed out of the stadium in St. Louis, I sat in awe as I watched Mark McGwire do what kids for a hundred years had dreamed about. The magic of that moment evoked memories of Johnny Bench and George Foster hitting balls out of Riverfront. I felt his exuberance as he ran past first base without touching it and then returned when the coach yelled at him to come back. The smile on his face brought back memories of the joy Pete Rose expressed after stealing second, and suddenly I was as excited and hopeful as I had been as a kid. For the first time since my husband and I split, my heart was overflowing with optimism. Throughout the divorce, I had forgotten that dreams every now and then do come true. Here, before my eyes, it was happening.

The following season I was ready to get out there again—to enjoy the city, find new activities, and create a new social network. I discovered that it took twenty minutes to get to Shea Stadium from my house in Brooklyn. On Friday nights when I wasn't working, I would zip out no matter whom the Mets were playing. I never got the best seat, but I often got good ones in the loge section or the mezzanine.

This single ticket would place me sitting in the fourth seat of a group of friends, or with an older gentleman who had once watched the Dodgers at Ebbets field. I was slowly immersing myself in the world of the Mets and even the Yankees, who had played such textbook baseball the previous year. They gave me something to root for locally. The fans around me were always surprised that I had come to the game alone, but they would quickly include me in their baseball chatter. Married gentlemen would tease me, telling me that they wished they had met me first, and we would all tell stories about our childhood baseball memories. Though Mets fans still resented the Reds for getting the better of the Seaver deal, by the end of the evening I always felt that I had made a few friends. I still think of some of them, like the old college buddies that came each year for the Mets-Cards series. Three of them were New York fans, and three were fans of the Redbirds. The guys whose team had lost the Friday game would have to wear the winners' hats the next day and so on through the weekend. These outings began to restore my confidence in myself, and the Mets mantra, "You gotta believe," coined by Tug McGraw during the 1973 season, restored my faith that I wasn't always going to be alone.

That winter I bought an apartment and began getting to know my neighborhood. I met people in the bar across the street, where I would go and shoot a little pool, and during baseball season they all came to know me as "the woman who likes baseball." The bar had satellite cable, and every now and then the old-timers would indulge my desire to see the Reds.

Misti Potter, a Braves fan, once told me, "A woman who can talk about sports can fit in with any group of men, and she will be welcome in any crowd." Women in business often find that if they can participate in sports conversations, even on a rudimentary level, they will be included more in the male-dominated activities. My ability to talk about the game has always helped me make contacts, and the one thing I learned while I was dating was that if the conversation dried up, I could easily bring it back to baseball (and in New York, to the pros and cons of the Yankees) and get through the evening. A teenage fan in Philly bemoaned the fact that she "wasn't brought up to be a baseball fan because she was a girl." Now, she felt she had to catch up to have stuff to talk about with her male friends.

Women respond to baseball for very different reasons than most men. In both St. Louis and Milwaukee, there are women who bring cookies to the relief pitchers in the bullpen. It's the idea of the team as a family that appeals to many women. The ladies who sit down the left-field line in the outfield at Pac Bell feel connected to the players and to the folks who sit around them, referring to them as "family." During my travels, the women I spoke to tended to tell me personal things about the players on the field, and frequently chose their favorite players by the sportsmanship that they demonstrated. The women who sat in front of me at the Cardinals game hissed when Reggie Sanders came to the plate. One explained her strong reaction: after Reggie had been brushed back by Matt Morris during a past game he made comments to the press about the Cardinals pitchers. During this game, he had been jawing a little, and she didn't like it one bit. "Matt Morris gets a little nervous when he's pitching," she explained. She didn't like Sanders messing with her pitcher, feeling she had to protect "her guys." This is not a recent phenomenon. In 1977, *Family Weekly* reported that Pearl Sandow, a Braves fan, "always cheers as her 'family' takes the field. Her family is the Atlanta Braves and she hasn't missed a game in eleven years."[17]

The idea of the team as a family has been hurt by free agency. The player movement of recent years has made it more difficult for people to identify with both individual players and teams. Many women, I think, want to feel a familiarity with the players, and they are drawn into the game only when the roster is stable and they can cheer for the same athletes every year. I would be lying if I said women didn't want to win as well. However, I think women have a more difficult time separating the men and their histories from their skills. Even I must admit I wanted the Cardinals to play the A's in the 2002 World Series mostly because I liked the idea of Yankees' Jason Giambi who came to the Yankees for a lot of money watching on television as his former team and the guy he replaced in New York played late in October. This seemingly mean-spirited desire was not the result of any dislike for the Yankee first baseman. It was just antipathy for the state of baseball today, when one still wishes that loyalty won championships.

I met a man in Minnesota who often appears in broadcasts sitting to the right of the first-base dugout. When purchasing season tickets, he had picked the seats closest to the field that also afforded him a good view into the Twins' dugout on the third-base side. He had become a fixture at the games, and everyone I spoke to prior to my first game recommended that I speak to him about his experiences. He was identified as the consummate Metrodome fan, and he lived up to his billing. When I approached him and introduced myself, he seemed excited to share his story. This professional architect was a recovering alcoholic who had moved to Minneapolis years earlier to take advantage of the city's fantastic drug and alcohol treatment center. He told me that a large part of his problem had been that he had enjoyed going to bars, where he saw familiar faces and people who were happy to see him. When beginning recovery, leaving this extended "family" behind was one of the most difficult things to do. He had always liked baseball, so he decided to get season tickets to fill the void he now felt. He soon came to a stunning realization: just like at the bar, here at the ball field he would see the same faces day after day. He began to see people he had talked to previously, and they would ask about him and his family. The sense of neighborhood and community he had experienced in the bar existed right here, at the game. The players are familiar with him as well, and even after they are traded they often stop by to say hello as members of the visiting team. For him, the stadium became the proverbial "place where everybody knows your name."

Rich Lamb, a Mets fan, pointed out another aspect of baseball in the modern era. The average fan over the past twenty years has had less and less leisure time to devote to following a team. "As an adult, a baseball team is harder to follow (and root for) when the rosters keep changing," he explained. This may also explain why football's popularity has grown. It is significantly easier to watch one game a week, not to mention digest the standings, read about injuries, and follow transactions, than it is to follow a season that lasts 162 games. We lose the sense of continuity, and it doesn't help matters that so many players change teams from year to year.

As computers have begun to detach us from our communities, people have sought ways to reach out to others in a safe environment. Sports can allow us to connect, to create surrogate communities. It isn't just the people on the field who validate our roles in society, but the people sitting next to us at the game as well. In fact, what connected me to the Mets for several years—as Steve Phillips, the former Mets general manager, performed one makeover after another—were the people sitting next to me in the stands. When I didn't renew my tickets for 2003, I soon realized I would miss them more than the action on the field.

The camaraderie that baseball inspires was exemplified by a group of gentleman I met in Colorado who were sitting next to me during breakfast at my hotel. I overheard them talking about the game against the Braves the night before and then other games that they had seen. I immediately recognized them as real fans of the game, and after speaking with them for a few minutes, I asked them to keep in touch so I could hear more about how they had gotten involved. One of the group, Rick Rapa, shared how the eleven men began getting together.

"We grew up together in Atlanta and most of us have known each other between twenty and thirty years. We've been playing baseball together since some of us were eight years old. We called ourselves the 'Stormers.' Legend has it that in the old days, when we got on the telephone to schedule a game, it was called 'storming the phone,' hence we became the Stormers. We played every summer until we were thirty years old. I am talking about every night, and sometimes doubleheaders on weekends. It was always hardball; even as we got older we never took the step back to softball. As we got older, some of the guys moved away (to Portland, Chicago Cleveland, Richmond, and so on). The guys who still live in Atlanta try to play at least one game a year to keep the tradition alive, though it is hard with wives, kids, and old age. About seven years ago, some of the guys decided to go on a road trip to Wrigley Field. Since then it had evolved into an annual pilgrimage to see the Braves in an out-of-town weekend series. We have been to New York, Boston, Philly, Denver, Milwaukee, and other towns. The game is a great way to keep in touch with the guys who have moved out of town, while feeding our hunger for baseball." For these men, it is the chance to meet and bond with friends who have grown and changed over the years that keeps the tradition alive. Others told me of how they still keep one eye on Atlanta despite forming allegiances to their new hometown clubs. Baseball has tied them not only to friends from long ago but also to the children that they once were.

Joe Balitewicz wrote, "Old Comiskey is where I grew up. I learned how to keep score, how to live with tragic losses, how to sneak beers, how to yell for peanuts, and how to sit in the sun with Harry Caray, who used to announce from the bleachers during the 1970s." Harry Kapsales remembers his older cousins visiting from Upstate NY: "Since, for some unknown reason, we didn't have a radio in the house, we would go out to the car and listen to the Yankee games there." Kyle, a Phillies fan, remembers his grandmother teaching him the rules during the World Series when he was five or six. Tom Malady talks about his father teaching him "the right way to keep score—all the different terminology, like 'can 'o corn,' 'Baltimore chopper,' 'bullpen,' and the great nicknames, like the 'Babe,' 'Iron Horse,' 'Three-Fingered Brown,' 'Joltin' Joe,' the 'Splendid Splinter' and 'Teddy Ballgame' (Ted had two), the 'Gashouse Gang' and the 'Say Hey Kid.'" Frank Imbarlina says, "I remember going to games and watching them on TV with my mother and father, having them explain the intricacies to me. My mom taught me how to keep score—she's a big fan."

Our first memories of baseball, especially those that involve our families, create our fondness for the sport. Teams have to make it easier for kids to see entire games with their parents, both in the stadium and on television.

On September 11, 2001, the world as I knew it changed. Living in New York on that day and in the days that followed, I experienced a range of emotions that I had never felt before. Fear and concern gradually gave way to an intense sense of gratitude. Though I wasn't near the buildings when they fell, I had a view of the towers from the building I was in, and I watched as one stood alone and then it too was gone. On my way home that day, after the subway reopened nearly eight hours later, while buildings still burned, I ran into people who had been there, who were still coated in ash, and who were not only struggling with what they had been through that day but also the simple issue of how they would get home that evening, to places like New Jersey and Staten Island. As we reentered Brooklyn on a very crowded train, everyone was silent. It was a silence I had never experienced in bustling New York. As my F train rose above ground, approaching the Smith and Ninth Street station, the crowd on the car began to lean towards the window, trying to get a glimpse of the skyline, so familiar to us yet so changed on this day. The hole in the skyline, and the smoke that was rising from it, caused us all to gasp simultaneously. That was the moment 9/11 became personal, when I realized that, even though I had been a transplant the day before, I now was a part of this city in a way I could never have imagined.

When I got home my roommate had the TV tuned to the only station that we could still receive. The antennae of the local stations had been on top of the tower; without cable, one had to rely on CBS and the single New Jersey PBS station that was transmitting ABC news. Without cable, that's all the news of the outside world that we had.

Baseball was cancelled for a week, as was football. Surrounded by sadness and tension, I felt that sports should continue quickly; the stress was too much to handle without our usual distractions. Then I heard Jason Seahorn talk about his need to heal. He couldn't go about business as usual when his business was just a game. I realized that he was right. Here, with my limited view of what was going on in the rest of the world, I couldn't realize how the attacks had hurt the entire country. Everyone was a part of the disaster.

Shea Stadium, as one of the largest open areas in the city, had been a major staging site for relief workers, and it was still needed even when baseball was to resume. There was also the security issue of bringing large crowds together in NYC so soon, while the government was still trying to sort out how the unthinkable had happened. The New York games were moved to other venues, and home games were swapped with away games to give the city more time.

Baseball resumed in New York on September 21. The Mets were playing the Atlanta Braves, Mets fans' most despised league rival. I already had tickets for that game, and I was anxious to go. I needed some relief, a little pleasure to make my daily routine more tolerable. My friend Brian and I arrived early, and the lines were very, very long. Everyone was searched, and everything was patted down. No coolers or containers of any kind were permitted; in fact, you couldn't bring in anything you couldn't wear. Even backpacks were being thrown away. Game time was delayed about forty-five minutes to allow the crowd to enter and security to do its job. The pre-game ceremonies included Marc Anthony singing the Star Spangled Banner, Diana Ross singing God Bless America, and a military band playing Amazing Grace, as well as a color guard and a presentation of the flag by members of the NYPD, FDNY, NYPA, and other emergency workers. We were handed small flags as we entered. Having never been one to wave a flag, I was surprised at my desire to extend my arm high into the air to show my support for the heroes of September 11 and for New York in general. The players stood along the baselines, and following the ceremony, instead of returning to their respective dugouts to prepare for the game, these archrivals sought out friends on the other team to hug and comfort. Just as New Yorkers had for two weeks, these players needed a chance to say, "I'm glad you are here and all right."

The game itself was great. The Mets took a 2-0 lead early and held it until the Braves tied it up in the middle innings. Despite the intense emotions, both teams were playing solid baseball. During the seventh-inning stretch, Liza Minelli came out to sing "New York, New York." By the second line of the song, the entire stadium was singing along loudly and chills covered my whole body. Even my friend, the most irreverent man I'd ever met, was singing along. Liza herself was so moved that, after the song, she turned towards the Mets dugout and reached out for Jay Payton, who was innocently warming up in the on-deck circle. To his surprise, she grabbed him and hugged him for quite awhile, and I believe he was a bit alarmed. The gesture was not lost on those in the stands: she was trying to hug all of New York.

When play resumed with the game still tied, the crowd grew nervous that the Mets might not win. New York needed to win, and not just because they trailed the Braves in the standings. In the bottom of the eighth, Mike Piazza came up to bat. He seemed to be the hero of this drama we were watching unfold, and now was his time to do the impossible. With a two-and-two count, he swung and hit the ball over the left-field wall. The crowd went crazy, and the Mets won 3-2.

The Mets lost the next two games of that series. I have often wondered if the Braves pitcher, realizing how exciting it would be for the Mets to win on this night—and maybe even overcome with emotion himself—gave Piazza a nice fat pitch. If he did, I'd say he did the right thing. Either way, the Mets became a part of me that night, and baseball had begun my healing. Pride joined the gamut of emotions that I had endured over the past few weeks.

Though I had loved working in theater production in the early years of my career, now it was a source of unhappiness. I was now an administrator, and instead of creating great art I was now worrying about what that art would cost. September 11 told me that life was too short to waste a day being unhappy, so I decided that the current season would be my last one, and that by September 11, 2002, I would move on. As discussions of contraction began in the off-season, I realized that I wanted to see each stadium before teams started to disappear. I felt that if I followed the voice in my head, some new employment opportunity would arise. I again heard Tug McGraw say, "You gotta believe."

During the weeks and months following the disaster, New Yorkers were reaching out to one another, often in subtle and unexpected ways. We shared our stories of that day and listened as others recounted their experiences. Wherever we turned we saw a friend we were glad to see, and when we heard about their experiences, we understood them. Slowly we began on the path back to normalcy.

As I traveled and met people at the games, I found that they were happy to talk baseball. They wanted to reach out and connect, and baseball made that very easy. In an age when urbanites don't speak to strangers, the subject of baseball allowed me to open up to people I'd never met, and vice versa. When they discovered I lived in New York, they often asked me the same question in hushed tones: "Were you there when *it* happened?" I would tell them that I was. Then the conversation would shift to what they had seen or heard, and they would ask me to tell my story. They wanted to connect to it in an intimate way, and I tried to do my part to satisfy this need—by recounting a story that hadn't made the papers or some fact an outsider to the city wouldn't have known. In Denver, people related it to Columbine; in Florida, to Hurricane Andrew. It wasn't that they didn't realize the differences; they were simply sympathizing in the best way they knew how. I would try to shift the conversation back to baseball, and almost always it easily went that way. Baseball was the common thread that sewed together all the people I met that summer. The need to connect to history and to each other through joy and tragedy is something that I discovered we all share. Whether it's a great team or a group of mediocre individuals, the people on the field become a part of those who watch them. After 162 games, the team becomes family.

8

Circling the Bases: Heading for Home

Safeco Field
Anaheim Angels @ Seattle Mariners
July 26, 2002,
Aisle 120, Row 32, Seat 10

Though the trip to see the Seattle Mariners was actually done in mid-July follow-ing the Royals, I decided that this team needed to be separated from the "Mid-western" teams and placed here, in the last chapter about the road trip. The Seattle Mariners were playing the Anaheim Angels for a weekend series.

The Mariners joined the American League as an expansion team in 1977, along with the Toronto Blue Jays, marking the second occasion the city would be granted a pro franchise. Seattle's first major-league club, the Pilots, entered as an expansion franchise in 1969, but they played only one year before being sold and moved to Milwaukee. The State of Washington sued Major League Baseball for reneging on its grant of a franchise to the area, insisting that MLB reimburse them the building costs of the Kingdome. By 1977, though, the population in Seattle had grown significantly and was now the home of many transplants from Eastern cities, so in hopes of settling the lawsuit, MLB granted Seattle a second franchise. In their inaugural season, the Mariners drew more than a million fans to the Kingdome, then home of the NFL's Seahawks, despite losing ninety-eight games. It would be fifteen years before they finished with a winning record.

In 1989, the farm system started to pay off. Ken Griffey Jr. entered the big leagues that year and Alex Rodriguez followed in 1990. Randy Johnson also arrived in 1989, via a trade with Montreal. Despite these additions, the team posted a losing record in 1992, and management was replaced, with Lou Piniella becoming the field manager in 1993. He guided the team through a string of successful seasons, culminating in their first post-season berth, in 1995.

In 1994, the Kingdome was declared unsafe due to falling tiles, and while it underwent repairs, the M's finished their season on the road. Due to the Mariners' success on the field, baseball gained popularity in the Northwest, and with the Kingdome falling down, talks of building a new stadium heated up. The King County executives formed a committee to assess the need for and cost of a new stadium, and though a county sales tax increase was defeated at the polls, the state legislature created a package of taxes and rebates that made it possible for the Mariners to build a new ballpark.

With the future looking bright and a comfortable new stadium on the way, Seattle fans began falling in love with their team. People that liked baseball but hated wasting their beautiful days and evenings inside the hideous Kingdome began to attend more games. Even more importantly, they began investing in season tickets. Purchasing season tickets at the Kingdome ensured higher placement on the list for season tickets at Safeco Field, the Mariners' future home. Generally, people were happy with their decision to purchase tickets early so they could reap the benefits in the new stadium, but for a few who sat in the center-field bleachers, the plan did not work out so well. One man had purchased seats in center field at the Kingdome to allow his young son to sit right behind Ken Griffey Jr., who was then the heir-apparent to the title of greatest center fielder ever. Safeco was built, though, without seats behind the center-field wall. Therefore, when seats were allotted in Safeco, the season ticket holders behind center field were not allowed to choose their seats until after the people in the other sections had chosen theirs. After years of sitting in the front row of the center field section, he was now in the back row of the right field section. Furious with the Mariners, he rarely spent his own money on tickets now, not wanting to give the organization any of his money (although he still made it out to a fair number of games).

Safeco is a beautiful field, very much in the style of Colorado's Coors Field. Some fans still question the cost of the retractable roof, as it was used only a couple of times in the first two years that Safeco was open. Though it drizzles in the early morning many days throughout the year, summer days are usually fair weathered in Seattle, and cover is rarely required.

Even though there were quite a few empty seats that day, tickets were hard to come by. Safeco had become a trendy place to be seen. A young woman whom I met later that evening told me that the center-field concourse area, which offers a great view of the game, was one of the best places to meet a potential date in Seattle. The stadium definitely seemed to have the youngest demographic of any in the majors.

In the sixth inning, the grounds crew comes out and does a dance routine to sweep the field, as they do in Yankee Stadium. However, in Seattle they feature new dance choreography each home stand, which is a refreshing change of pace from the YMCA routine Yankee fans have had to endure for more than ten years now.

The M's were still atop the West at this point in 2002, but Anaheim was coming on strong and had just passed Oakland to move into second place, meaning this series could determine a new leader of the AL West. In fact, during these two games, it became apparent how much fight the Angels had in them, while it seemed the Mariners had become complacent as defending division champs. In fact, the Friday night game reminded me of my first game that season, when I watched the Blue Jays overpower the Devil Rays. The Angels scored three runs in the fourth, one in the fifth, three more in the sixth, and finally one more in the eighth—all unanswered. The Mariners pitching looked weak, its fielding seemed lackadaisical, and the batters were just plain bad. They rebounded for a win on Saturday, but it was a slim 3-1 victory. John Olerud walked in the second and scored on a double by Ruben Sierra, and then Edgar Martinez hit a two-run home run off of Jarrod Washburn in the fourth for his only hit. Despite the loss, the Angels seemed like a team rather than just a collection of players, which the M's dugout resembled. I therefore wasn't surprised two years later when the Mariners finished with one of the worst records in baseball.

During the second game, I had the good fortune to sit next to John Hickey, a sports columnist for the *Seattle Post-Inquirer.* This gentleman was generous enough to talk with me about the local fans. He said that while the local crowd was greatly disenchanted with the Sonics and the Seahawks, they would remain loyal to the Mariners, even though the team hadn't made the playoffs that year and Lou Piniella had departed. Baseball had the strongest footing of all the pro sports here, he felt. The crowds I saw did seem to love baseball. I had expected the late-to-arrive-early-to-leave types, much like I'd seen at other West Coast stadiums, but I was pleasantly surprised to see everyone in their seats at Safeco when the first pitch was thrown. Baseball really does have a foothold here. Now that they are no longer contenders, however, the Mariners will have to work hard to maintain the loyal fans they have created. They do seem to be trying, by making big moves in each off-season in attempt to regain their previous success.

Oriole Park at Camden Yards
Detroit Tigers @ Baltimore Orioles
August 17, 2002,
Section 46, Row RR, Seat 5

Baltimore followed closely on the heels of the series in Chicago, Milwaukee, and Minnesota. The original Orioles franchise, as part of the National League, won three consecutive pennants from 1894 to 1896. That strong team, which included Willie Keeler, Joe Kelley, Dan Brouthers, and John McGraw, was unmatched. In 1898, the owners of the Brooklyn Dodgers and the Orioles each purchased interests in the other's team in an effort to maximize the earnings of both clubs. The strongest players were transferred from the "small market" city of Baltimore to New York City in order to boost ticket sales in the larger market. With all of the talent now in Brooklyn, the Baltimore club quickly fell apart. Eventually, joint ownership was disallowed and the team was sold. They moved to New York, where they played as the Highlanders and, eventually, the Yankees. Though there were attempts to put another major-league team in Baltimore, the city wouldn't see pro baseball again until the St. Louis Browns moved to town in 1954, beginning a second Orioles era.

With the help of Brooks Robinson, Boog Powell, and the newly acquired Frank Robinson, the O's won the World Series in 1966. This, however, was only the beginning. Three years later, under the stewardship of Earl Weaver, the team would go onto win three consecutive pennants and the 1970 World Series. They returned to the World Series in 1979 but lost to Pittsburgh in seven games. They won their third championship against the Phillies in 1983, with the help of Eddie Murray and Cal Ripken Jr. Ripken went on to break Lou Gehrig's consecutive game streak, finishing his own streak in 1997 at 2,632 when he voluntarily removed himself from the lineup for the last home game of the season.

The Orioles moved from their original home at Memorial Stadium in 1992 to beautiful Oriole Park at Camden Yards. Camden Yards was one of first of the "new" stadiums, following on the heels of the New Comiskey. Its designers created the antique feel while installing state-of-the-art amenities, thereby setting the standard for all new parks to follow. The park doesn't seem extraordinary nowadays, but when I attended the second game ever played at the park years ago, I was captivated by its beauty. It was a refreshing and joyful experience.

On this mid-August day, the team was facing the Detroit Tigers. The O's had been playing poorly and were well out of the post-season race this season. The

Tigers were in even worse shape. This wasn't the series that I had wanted to see, but with the strike talks heating up I was afraid I'd lose my chance to see them play, so I bought my $35 ticket. An Orioles game is one of the more expensive tickets around, which surprised me. I was also surprised by the number of people in attendance for both games, considering the match-up; however, I found that most were either from out of town or season ticket holders. Many sported Cal Ripken Jr. shirts and jerseys, and the fans there seemed to be holding onto him as a remnant of their last great baseball moment. Ripken is still a local hero and he remains affiliated with the Orioles organization.

The stadium itself is another source of pride for Baltimore fans. As the trendsetter in stadium design, it has brought a great deal of attention to the city of Baltimore. It also didn't hurt that the O's became a highly competitive team in the mid-nineties not long after its opening, its highlight being Call Ripken Jr. and "The Streak." It is, without a doubt, a record that will never be broken. Perhaps even more than St. Louis, Baltimore is a baseball town that lives and dies by the legacies of its brightest stars.

The entire feel of baseball in Baltimore harkens back to times past. Though there is no shortage of things to do in Camden, baseball remains the focus. The food is better than you'd find in those older buildings, however, and one can even visit with Boog Powell as he sits by his barbecue stand past right field on most game days. Off the field, the Orioles take great care to draw a line from its past to its present. In addition to Powell, the O's television announcers in 2002 were Hall of Fame pitcher Jim Palmer and Cy Young winner Mike Flanagan. In 2003, Flanagan was brought into the general manager's office to work alongside Jim Beattie as co-GM.

The games I saw were not very memorable. The Orioles won the first 6-3 despite a strong outing by Mark Redman of the Tigers. The second game, on a ninety-nine-degree day, the Orioles lost 9-7 with the Tigers scoring at least one run in six of the nine innings. Five Baltimore pitchers combined to give up seventeen hits and five walks while striking out only five. The attendance for the first game was 34,000 while at the second it dipped to just over 30,000. Although those numbers represented tickets sold, they didn't seem to be too far off the number of people in the seats. To me, this offered hope to the new expansion franchises as well as the old teams that were struggling. Loyalty can be won, but the team has to work at it. What happens "between the lines" is important in creating new fans, but the Orioles proved that if a club plans on creating and maintaining a *community* of fans, it must provide both fine amenities and cultivate nostalgia for baseball history.

Minute Maid Park
Cincinnati Reds @ Houston Astros
August 23, 2002,
Section 120, Row 27, Seat 16

The Texas teams were next in line. I'd visit Houston first, to see a series against my Cincinnati Reds. Though I would find it tough to root for the home team, the fans around me were so pleasant and enthusiastic that I got caught up in their excitement by the end. The Astros home, formerly Enron Field but renamed Minute Maid Park after the Enron debacle, has a retractable roof and a glass wall along the outfield. This glass wall allows plenty of natural light to stream in, giving the park a more natural feel, especially during day games. Considering the Texas heat, this seemed to be the best compromise possible. With the roof closed, the stadium does feel a bit like a warehouse though—the building is rectangular in shape, and the roof and walls are constructed from cold, industrial-looking materials. The team usually opens the roof for night games in about the seventh or eighth inning, and when they do the atmosphere changes dramatically. The field is bright, and the seating bowl is designed so that the focus is on the action, which is very important for me. It's only when you step back and look across from one concession area to the other that one gets the idea that baseball is actually manufactured here.

I sat next to some very friendly fans during the Friday-night game. Paul was originally from California, but he had lived in the Baltimore area long enough to have adopted the Orioles. After living in Houston for a number of years, his allegiance had shifted again, to the Astros. He was a true baseball fan who enjoyed the game on many different levels: he relished his experiences as a child, he used baseball as a means to keep in touch with old friends (calling them on the phone during games), and he had established ties to his new community through the sport after moving to Houston. He spoke about the Astros with genuine enthusiasm, especially regarding the things the team had gotten right recently, including the atmosphere and location of their building.

At this point in the 2002 season, the Astros had no hopes of making the playoffs. They had suffered quite a few injuries, and though they had been able to bring some young players up from the minors, the team had underachieved this year. Despite the disappointment that many fans expressed, there were 37,000 of them in attendance that Friday night. On Sunday, I arrived at the park before the gates opened. While in line, I struck up a conversation with the gentleman in front of me about the history of the Astros. He had been an Astro fan from day one, when the team was formed as an expansion franchise in 1962, when they played as the Colt .45s.

In 1965, the Colt .45s become the Houston Astros and began play inside the first indoor baseball stadium, the Astrodome, known as the "Eighth Wonder of the World." The Astros put together many successful seasons throughout the 1960s and 1970s, with strong individual performances from players such as Joe Morgan, Larry Dierker, Cesar Cedeno, and Joe Niekro; however, it wasn't until 1980, eighteen years after the team's inception, that they finally appeared in the post-season, after defeating Los Angeles in a one-game playoff.

They made a second appearance in the split season of 1981, while Nolan Ryan threw his record fifth no-hitter that year. With the Astros, Ryan would go on to pass Walter Johnson's all-time strikeout mark and, later, to become the first player ever to record 4,000 strikeouts. The 1980s for the Astros were marked by some outstanding pitching performances, not only by Ryan but also by All-Star Mike Scott, Houston's first Cy Young Award winner. The teams of the mid-1990s had a lot of promise. After losing the wild-card spot to Colorado by one game in 1995, the Astros came back to win their division in 1997, and then again in 1998 and 1999. During that run, Craig Biggio and Jeff Bagwell had several outstanding seasons, setting a number of records.

The team moved into their new stadium in 2000. The newer, smaller field allowed the Astros to set numerous individual and club home-run records, but the team finished below .500 for the first time since 1991. Houston returned to the post-season in 2001 with another division win, but once again they were unable to proceed past the first round. In 2004 they created a buzz by signing free agent Andy Pettitte and luring recent retiree Roger Clemens back to the game. Though Pettitte finished the season on the disabled list, the Astros won the wild card. They also managed to win their first post-season series ever, beating the Braves to move on to the NLCS, where they lost to the Cardinals.

The fans in Houston are very loyal. Like fans of many teams with a history of losing big games, Astros fans cling to the hope that their boys will pull through for them one day. They also still have strong athletes who play the game well, namely Biggio, Bagwell, but others too. The team seems to be loaded with heart, which is important to loyal Texan fans. Astros management also seems committed to winning, making trades and bringing up players from the farm system every year to assemble the strongest nine possible. The two Texas teams seem isolated from the rest of the baseball world, both geographically and in spirit. Texans are proud of their local heritage and distinct culture, and they have forged a bond with their baseball club that will help ensure the Astros thrive in Houston for many years to come.

The Ballpark at Arlington
Baltimore Orioles @ Texas Rangers
August 27, 2002,
Section 327, Row 3, Seat 2

Arlington, Texas, the home of the Texas Rangers, was the next stop. The Rangers originally began as the second incarnation of the Washington Senators, after the original Senators, owned by Calvin Griffith, moved to Minnesota and became the Twins. General Elwood Quesada was granted a franchise to begin play in Washington in 1961. MLB began looking into the viability of baseball in the Dallas-Fort Worth area at the end of the 1962 season, when Charley Finley, owner of the Kansas City A's, attempted to move his franchise there. He was voted down, but the idea of a team relocating there continued to resurface. Before the 1963 season, three Texas businessmen bought Quesada's shares in the Senators and began building a ballpark for a club in the Texas League, a branch of the minor-league system. Ownership would change again when Robert E. Short, the Democratic National Committee Chairman, purchased majority shares of the team in 1968. In 1971, he received permission to move the franchise to Arlington, Texas, for the 1972 season, and the Texas Rangers were born. Expansion began on the minor-league ballpark to accommodate the new big-league team. In their second year in Texas, the Rangers recorded their first no-hitter, when Jim Bibby shut out the Oakland A's. They also had their First Rookie of the Year, when Mike Hargrove took home the honor for the American League.

In 1974, ownership changed as a group led by Bradford G. Corbett's purchased the club. He would last only six years as owner before selling the team in 1980 to H. E. Chiles. Arlington Stadium, which was owned by the city, underwent renovations to accommodate 42,000 fans in 1976. In 1983, the city of Arlington signed over complete control of the facility to the Rangers organization. The team purchased the stadium outright in 1987. In 1989, Rangers changed ownership again, when a group headed by George W. Bush and Edward W. Rose purchased controlling interests in the club.

The Rangers signed Nolan Ryan as a free agent before the 1989 season. When he struck out Rickey Henderson on August 22, 1989, he became the first pitcher ever to record 5,000 strikeouts. Against the same team the following June, he recorded his sixth no-hitter. In July, he won his 300th game. In 1991, he threw his seventh no-hitter, setting a major-league record by becoming the oldest pitcher ever to record one. Ryan retired after the 1993 season and went into the Hall of Fame in 1999, becoming the first player to do so as a Texas Ranger.

In 1990, the Rangers announced plans to build a ballpark adjacent to Arlington Stadium. The following year the city approved a one-half-cent tax to finance municipal bonds for the ballpark, offering up to 135 million dollars in financial support. The Ballpark at Arlington opened in 1994. Midway through that season, the Rangers recorded their first perfect game, when Kenny Rogers beat the Orioles 4-0. The Rangers finally made their first post-season appearance in 1996, though they lost the Division Series to the New York Yankees. Juan Gonzalez was chosen the AL's Most Valuable Player, and Johnny Oates was named Manager of the Year. In 1998, the club was sold again, this time to local businessman Thomas Hicks. That year, the Rangers returned to the post-season, again losing to the Yankees in three games in the Division Series. Juan Gonzalez won his second MVP Award in 1999. In 2000, the Rangers made history by signing Alex Rodriguez to the most lucrative contract in professional sports history, a ten-year deal worth $252 million.

In their thirty-two-year history, the Texas Rangers have managed to finish above the .500 mark only twelve times. They have won ninety or more games only three times. They have had eighteen different managers and six different ownership groups. If Alex Rodriguez had played out his contract with the Rangers, he would have been with the team longer than any owner except the one who signed him, assuming that Mr. Hicks didn't sell the team in the meantime. Stability has not been a hallmark of the team's history.

It's common for new owners who have had success in other arenas to carry over the lessons they've learned into baseball. Hicks believed that the best way to begin his tenure as Rangers owner was to make a big statement by signing a high-profile free agent, which he did when he inked Rodriguez to his monumental deal. Hicks not only landed a great player with the potential to become the cornerstone of the franchise, but he also managed to create an enormous buzz. Suddenly, the Texas Rangers were being mentioned in the same breath as the New York Yankees. However, hindsight has shown that Hicks may have miscalculated. Buzz does not win ball games, and neither does one player. Though local fans were originally excited about the big splash and ownerships desire to put the Rangers on the map, they soon became disenchanted by the string of unsuccessful seasons and the idea of one contract impairing their team's ability to fill holes on the roster. Prior to the 2004 season, the team traded Rodriguez to the Yankees for several players. The move paid off, and the Rangers quickly moved to the top of their division. In 2002, however, the fans in the stands had grown distrustful of ownerships choices, and that trust could be hard to win back.

The Rangers' ticket prices in 2002 reflected a "big-market" payroll, but not the community or its needs. A box seat in the upper deck cost $16 at the Ballpark at Arlington. The same seat at Turner Field, in Atlanta, where the team had won their division every year for the past thirteen years, had cost only $12. The games I watched in Arlington were unspectacular. Alex Rodriguez did make one great catch—a barehanded grab of a drive up the middle that he threw on the fly for the out at first—and he did hit a two-run home run, leading the Rangers to a 9-4 win over the Orioles, but I'd be hard pressed to say the experience was worth $16.

The amenities at the Ballpark also leave a lot to be desired. There was only one concession area open upstairs, but even it had closed down by the fifth inning. The fans, who had overpaid for their tickets, weren't even being served. Most moved downstairs, but if they were "caught" by an usher they were instructed to return to their original seats. The upper deck should have been closed. Attendance was announced at 20,139, but there couldn't have been more than 12,000 in the park.

Mr. Hicks approach to ownership thus far has been to treat his club like a brand-new expansion franchise. While this may provide excitement for the fans in the short term, he will soon learn the lessons that all expansion owners must learn once the novelty of their clubs wears off. The Orioles were in a similar position after Peter Angelos bought the team and flooded his team with big contracts from the free-agent market. Years later, they were still paying for Albert Belle. Mr. Angelos has learned his lesson, and so will Mr. Hicks.

The ballpark itself is quite lovely. It sits off the highway, up on a hill, and looks almost like a well-fortified castle from the outside. Its sides are covered with reliefs depicting monumental events in Texas history. The inside reminds one of Camden Yards, though instead of an old brick warehouse past the outfield wall there is a building that looks somewhat like a riverboat. There is also a bit of trim around the upper deck, reminding one of Yankee Stadium. It is a very comfortable and roomy stadium, though it may have merely seemed so because the building was so empty the day I was there. The only food available was traditional ballpark fare. Considering the price of tickets, one would expect a lot more.

Two days following my visit to Arlington, MLB announced that the players and owners had come to an agreement, putting an end to the strike talk. This marked the first time since the first CBA was signed that the two sides had reached an agreement without a work stoppage. Most fans were relieved that they would not need to follow through on their threats to cut baseball out of their lives if a work stoppage did occur, but quite a few felt the last-minute nature of the deal had sullied baseball's reputation once again. My biggest concern had been that I wouldn't get to see all of the teams, that all my work would be in vain because I wouldn't complete the trip. I had to believe they wouldn't strike; I had to believe I had been able to overcome my self-doubt for a reason.

I had asked anyone and everyone who knew about baseball what they thought the outcome would be. In Houston, I had asked Marty Brennaman, the broadcaster for the Reds, who told me he didn't believe there would be a strike. Sidney Ponson, a pitcher with the Orioles, had told me in Minnesota they were definitely striking, while in Texas he told me they definitely weren't. Coaches and trainers had shared their concerns, but of course they had the least say of all in the outcome. In Texas, Sid Thrift, the GM for the Orioles, had asked *me* about what others were saying. In the end, the fans were happy that they would be able to enjoy a day at the ballpark for years to come. To me, it also meant that I would be able to finish this project.

PNC Park
Florida Marlins @ Pittsburgh Pirates
September 6, 2002,
Section 120, Row Q, Seat 10

I was off to Pittsburgh next to see the Pirates, a team for which I felt great nostalgia, since they were inextricably linked to my memories of baseball as a kid and the Reds' drive to the World Series in 1990. Three Rivers Stadium was also more similar to my Riverfront than any other park, and though it was no longer around, I was filled with anticipation to see what had replaced it. What I found could very well be the crown jewel of baseball parks.

As opposed to the antiseptic and cavernous Three Rivers, PNC Park was intimate, comfortable, and reminiscent of an easier, simpler time. It honored its community both by providing a spectacular view of beautiful downtown Pittsburgh from the outfield and by featuring decorative steel construction inside, a nod to the industry that has helped Pittsburgh thrive in the twentieth century.

Whereas Comerica Park in Detroit sets you away from the players, PNC put you in the center of the action, and you feel as if you can reach out and touch any of the ballplayers from any seat. The food choices were much more diverse than I found in other Midwestern parks. Both the food and the beer selections represented the local flavors of Pittsburgh, as did the "Pirogue Race," which features pirogues racing along the stands in foul territory, a local variation of Milwaukee's Sausage Race.

The games against the Florida Marlins, which took place in the first week of September, were not critical to the standings, nor did they draw big crowds. The fans in the stands, though, were no less enthusiastic. Several sported the flat-top Pirates caps of the 1970s. Others could tell you the history of the team in detail. The Pirates honor their history throughout the stadium, with statues of Honus Wagner, Roberto Clemente, and Willie Stargell outside. Also, one must take a ride across the Roberto Clemente Bridge to get from downtown to the ballpark, a really relaxing approach.

The history of the team goes back to the founding of the National League, when they played as the Pittsburgh Alleghenies. They were dubbed the Pirates two years later after "stealing" Louis Bierbauer away from the Philadelphia Athletics. In 1900, the owner of the former Louisville club bought controlling interest in the Pirates and brought Honus Wagner with him from Kentucky. Behind Wagner, who hit .353 and drove in 126 runs, the Buccaneers won the pennant in 1901, as well as in 1902 and 1903, when they went on to lose in the first ever World Series, to the Boston Americans (later known as the Red Sox). In 1909, Forbes Field opened, becoming the first stadium made from steel and poured concrete. They won the World Series that year, against Ty Cobb's Detroit Tigers. In 1921, the Pirates and Phillies played the first game ever to be carried over the radio waves, by KDKA of Pittsburgh. The Pirates returned to the World Series in 1925, beating the Senators, but lost two years later to Babe Ruth's Yankees. Honus Wagner was elected to the Baseball Hall of Fame in 1936, becoming one of the first five players ever inducted into the Hall.

The Pirates wouldn't return to the World Series until 1960, when they would avenge the loss of the 1927 team against the Yankees, with Bill Mazeroski hitting the game-winning home run in the bottom of the ninth inning of game seven. Three Rivers Stadium replaced Forbes Field in 1970, and the Pirates began a successful run, winning the World Series in 1971 against Baltimore. In 1972, 1974, and 1975, they won their division but lost in the National League Championship Series. In 1979, they returned to the October Classic against Baltimore and won in seven games. The years 1990 through 1992 also would see the Pirates win their division, though they never proceeded to the World Series. Unfortunately, due to their budgetary constraints, Pittsburgh lost much of its young talent to free agency. In the late 1990s, the team reversed this trend by signing several young players to large long-term contracts. This too turned out to be a mistake, as the market changed and none of the players they signed quite lived up to their potential. The team was saddled with a number of cumbersome contracts and lacked the flexibility to go after the players they needed.

In a city whose biggest industry has suffered from severe cutbacks and whose population has declined over the past three decades, how can an old NL team hope to compete? Even now, many feel, the only reason ownership hasn't relocated the Pirates is because of the loyalty they feel towards the community. Though the team has started off very strong over the last three years, they haven't been able to sustain the momentum into the second half, likely a result of the team's youth. This problem will continue until they are able to sign free-agent veterans and keep their young talent. Without that, the most beautiful stadium in the major leagues will be nearly empty. Pittsburgh has the most to lose as the gulf grows between big- and small-market teams, and they perhaps best exemplify the perils of the free market in the modern age of baseball. Though its history is one of the richest in baseball, the Pirates are one of the poorest teams in terms of dollars and cents, and they are now trying to rebuild as a first-year expansion franchise might do.

Fenway Park
Baltimore Orioles @ Boston Red Sox
September 13, 2002,
Section 16, Row 01, Seat 1

The Boston Red Sox are one of only four original American League teams that remain in the cities where they began, along with Detroit, Cleveland, and Chicago. Their history begins with a list of great stars, including "Cy" Young and Tris Speaker. Behind these athletes, the Americans, as they were then called, went to the first World Series in 1903 and beat the Pittsburgh Pirates. In 1907, the Boston NL franchise changed its name from the Red Stockings to the Doves and changed the team colors from red to blue. The owner of the AL franchise, John I. Taylor, adopted the now-available red color scheme and changed the name of his team to the Red Sox. Fenway opened in 1912, and the Red Sox won the American League pennant and World Series that year, behind pitcher Smokey Joe

Wood. Babe Ruth joined the team in 1914, and the newly dubbed Red Sox went on to win the World Series in 1915, 1916, and 1918. Unfortunately, owner Harry Frazee sold Ruth and many others to the Yankees in order to fund a production of *No, No Nanette*.

The Sox didn't finish above .500 in any season in the 1920s. Frazee sold the team to Bob Quinn, who in turn sold it to Tom Yawkey in 1933. Fire had destroyed part of Fenway under Quinn, and Yawkey needed to rebuild both the bleachers and the team. In 1934, Joe Cronin became player-manager and Jimmie Foxx and Lefty Grove both had career years in 1938. Ted Williams joined the team in 1939. In 1941, Williams would bat .406 and Grove would pick up his 300th win. Along with Dom DiMaggio and Johnny Pesky, Williams made the 1940s a memorable time in Boston, leading them back to the World Series in 1946. They lost to the St. Louis cardinals in seven games. Two years later, they lost a one-game playoff for the pennant to the Cleveland Indians.

The 1950s and 1960s brought many more great individual performances. Walter Dropo won Rookie of the Year in 1950; Frank Malzone won three gold gloves in 1957, 1958, and 1959; and Don Schwall would win Rookie of the Year honors in 1961. Pumpsie Green joined the team in 1959, becoming the first black player to play for the Red Sox, who were the last team to integrate. Ted Williams retired in 1960, hitting a home run in his last at-bat, and Carl Yastrzemski would take his place in left field the following year. In 1967, Yastrzemski won the Triple Crown as well as league MVP, and Jim Lonborg captured the Cy Young Award while leading the team to a World Series appearance against St. Louis. St. Louis won, again in seven games.

The 1970s Red Sox featured stars such as Carlton Fisk, Luis Tiant, Fred Lynn, and Jim Rice. In 1975, they went back to the World Championship Series against the Cincinnati Reds. Again, they lost the series in seven games, but it will always be remembered for a twelve-inning marathon in game six that ended with one of the greatest moments in the history of the game. Carlton Fisk hit a shot to left field, and as he ran up the line he waved his arms furiously, motioning for the ball to stay fair. The ball hit the left-field foul pole and sent the Series to game seven. That clip, which was only accidentally caught on tape by the cameraman, became one of the most enduring images of the modern era, and it appears on highlight reels to this day.

The Red Sox returned to the World Series in 1986, behind Cy Young Award winner and MVP Roger Clemens. They lost again in seven games, this time to the New York Mets. Clemens would win his second Cy Young Award the following year, though the team wouldn't fair as well. The team finished first in their division in both 1988 and 1990, but they were defeated in the American League Championship Series by the Oakland A's both times. Mrs. Jean Yawkey passed away in 1992, sixteen years after her husband, and ownership of the team passed to the Yawkey Trust, headed by her partners, John L. Harrington and Haywood C. Sullivan. Sullivan sold his shares to the Trust in 1993, leaving Harrington to run the organization. The Red Sox had great success at the end of the 1990s, reaching the post-season in 1995, 1998, and 1999, and with the additions of Nomar Garciaparra in 1997 and Pedro Martinez in 1998, the Sox were able to make it past the Division Series in 1999, only to lose in the ALCS to the New York Yankees. Martinez won the Cy Young Award that year, a feat he repeated in 2000.

The rivalry for the American League East between New York and Boston was strong throughout 2003. The Sox won the AL wild card race but lost to the Yankees in dramatic fashion, courtesy of an extra-innings home run off the bat of Aaron Boone. Finally, in 2004, the Red Sox ended their drought: they came back from a 3-0 deficit to beat the Yankees in the ALCS, and then went on to beat the Cardinals in the World Series.

Fenway Park, the oldest serving major-league baseball stadium—Tiger Stadium opened the same year and is still in use, though not by the Tigers—is a truly special place to see a baseball game. Its concourse areas are dank, unpleasant, and difficult to navigate, but upon stepping into the seating area, one finds oneself in a cozy and intimate setting unlike any other in baseball. The Green Monster, the tall left-field wall, was so close to the backstop that it seemed impossible to have been built for major-league play. Like Pittsburgh, the place felt intimate, and like Yankee Stadium, the history of the place overwhelmed me. The fans in Boston love their Red Sox, but in the last two weeks of the 2002 season they were more than a little upset with their team's inability to challenge the Yankees for the division title. Players were not running out ground balls; in fact, days before, Manny Ramirez hadn't even left the batter's box after hitting one.

Boston fans aren't shy about sharing their point of view. Even though they were hosting the lackluster Baltimore Orioles, the stands were packed. The Red Sox were a huge part of these fans' lives, and they seemed more hopeful than ever that the Sox might win it all someday soon. The wild card was still a possibility that year, but it was quite a long shot. While the dreams of Sox fans went unanswered that season, two years later they would be fulfilled in a way that the long-suffering fans in Fenway scarcely could have imagined. Again, baseball taught us that dreams can come true.

Cinergy Field
Pittsburgh Pirates @ Cincinnati Reds
September 20, 2002,
Aisle 116, Row 29, Seat 101

The last team I would see on my journey, my team, the Cincinnati Reds, were closing the ballpark in which I had grown up. The new park was nearly finished, and they had planned festivities for the final series at Riverfront/Cinergy Field against the Philadelphia Phillies. Friday night was a rainout, so Saturday would become a double header, which the Reds would lose entirely. The place was packed, though, as it had often been in my youth. Fans had come from far away just to see the old stadium one last time, the same fans who had cheered for the team throughout the 1970s.

The Reds may be the team with the oldest demographic as their fan base, a problem many teams face when they have gone through long periods between championships. The sports radio programs were filled with callers wanting to share stories—many involving the ways they had snuck into the stadium as children but also some recalling Pete Rose's hit that broke Ty Cobb's record, or Tom Browning's perfect game. People were more than glad to tell me who their favorite player had been, and much like in St. Louis and Anaheim, the choices ran the gamut—from Lee May to Johnny Bench.

The club did a wonderful job celebrating the thirty years they had spent at Riverfront. Saturday night there was a fireworks show accompanied by a historical soundtrack including sound bytes from Marty Brennaman's and Joe Nuxhall's broadcasts. As I am a sucker for any documentary about baseball, I listened with fondness as the familiar voices brought back memories of great Reds moments. I had chills and my eyes welled up with tears. This season, baseball had become as central to my life as it had been when I sat in the seats at Riverfront as a kid. The crowd ooohed and aaahed, and even though the Reds had lost both games that day, they left feeling the high they had grown accustomed to in the Reds' better days.

The Reds history is marked by waves of success followed by years of stagnation. In 1869, the Cincinnati Reds Stockings became the first openly professional team, playing its entire season with its whole roster under contract. The total payroll was $11,000, with George Wright, the star shortstop, making $2000 that year. After the 1870 season, the team was disbanded after losing too much money.

When the modern National League was founded, the Reds became charter members. In 1880, the National League kicked the Reds out of the league for selling beer and allowing amateur teams to play baseball on its grounds on Sundays, both practices having been banned by the league. In response, the Reds helped found the American Association, the first league to compete successfully with the National League, a legitimate second "major league." Though the Reds had success with the American Association, the league itself was disbanded in 1890 as many teams either suffered financial losses or were lured back to the National League. Over the next twenty-nine years, the Reds would never finish higher than third place. Opening day was a big tradition during this era, as there was not much to get excited about throughout the season. A parade became part of the tradition, and to this day the city of Cincinnati nearly closes down in order to celebrate opening day. For many years there was an unwritten rule that the first pitch to be thrown in any ballpark in the majors was to be thrown in Cincinnati. In the last few years that has gone by the wayside, with games now taking place overseas a week earlier than the normal start of the season, but the Reds are still given the honor of opening their season at home.

After joining the NL, the Reds' next winning season didn't come until 1919, when they beat the New York Giants for the pennant. Despite Cincinnati's .686 winning percentage that season, the Reds were the underdogs in the World Series. They ended up beating the Chicago White Sox that year in the best-of-nine series, but a year later, eight members of the Chicago team were accused of participating in a plot to fix the Series. Those eight, known as the Black Sox, were banned from baseball for life.

At the end of the 1920s the team was sold, and the new owner, Sidney Weill, lost most of his money in the stock market crash of 1929. The Reds suffered for a few years, and Weill was forced to sell the team to Powell Crosley. Crosley immediately changed the name of Redland Field, the stadium where the Reds played, to Crosley Field and hired Larry McPhail to fix the faltering franchise. McPhail introduced night baseball in Cincinnati on May 24, 1935, in front of more than 20,000 fans. The Reds played seven night games that year, averaging 18,000 fans a night (versus the daytime average of 4,600). In 1938, Johnny Vander Meer set a major-league record by pitching two consecutive no-hitters. That year, the Reds also got a new field manager, Bill McKechnie, who led the club from eighth place to fourth. The next year, they won the pennant but lost to the Yankees in four games, with Joe DiMaggio scoring the go-ahead run in the tenth inning of game seven. The Reds returned to the World Series the following year, led by Bucky

Walters and Paul Derrringer, who combined for four complete-game victories to win the Series in seven games.

The Reds then started to lag, and with World War II taking most players, the Reds went looking for anyone who could play. They recruited fifteen-year-old high school pitcher Joe Nuxhall from nearby Hamilton, Ohio. He still holds the record for the youngest player ever to appear in a game, and he is now also the person with the longest association with one team, as he still works for the Reds almost sixty years later.

The 1950s passed uneventfully, with the exceptions of Ted Kluszewski and Frank Robinson. Klu, as he was called, led the league in home runs and RBI in 1954. Following the 1956 season, Frank Robinson became the Reds' first Rookie of the Year. That year, the team tied the major-league home run record with 221. The Reds also underwent a nickname change to avoid any suspicion of ties to the Communist Party. For this short time they were known as the Redlegs. By the 1960's, the scare had passed, and they took up their old moniker.

Paul Crosley died in 1960 and a new owner, Bill Dewitt, took over. Under his ownership and with new field management, the Reds won the pennant in 1961, but they lost to the New York Yankees in the World Series. The Reds traded away Frank Robinson, but a number of talented young stars would soon make their debut on the roster, including Pete Rose, Lee May, Johnny Bench, and Tony Perez. Jim Maloney also threw three no-hitters in the 1960s.

The Reds were sold again in the late 1960s to ownership that was friendlier to a move to a multipurpose stadium. Cincinnati had acquired an NFL franchise and the city wanted to build one stadium for both teams. With George "Sparky" Anderson added as field manager the Reds began to build on the successes of the 1960s. They won the pennant in 1970 but lost to Frank Robinson and the Baltimore Orioles in the Series. In 1972, the Reds traded with the Astros to acquire Joe Morgan, Jack Billingham, Cesar Geronimo, and Denis Menke, and again they won the pennant. That year they lost the World Series to the Oakland A's, who would also win the next two October Classics. They came close to winning the pennant in 1973 and 1974, but they lost both years to the Mets and Dodgers respectively. In 1975, however, they won 108 games to secure a berth in the post season and beat the Boston Red Sox in a hotly contested seven games. In 1976, they won 102 games and then went on to sweep the New York Yankees in the World Series. The 1976 Reds led the major leagues in ten offensive, defensive, and pitching categories—runs scored, doubles, triples, home runs, batting average, slugging average, stolen bases, fewest errors, fielding percentage, and saves. By the end of the 1970s, the Reds' starting eight had earned six MVP awards, twenty-six Gold Gloves, and sixty-three All-Star selections, and the name the "Big Red Machine."

The beginning of the eighties would mark the end of the Reds' dominance, and management began dismantling the Machine. Perez was traded, Sparky Anderson was fired, and Rose was lost to free agency. In 1981, the Reds had the best record in baseball, but they failed to make a post-season appearance due to the strike and the subsequent split season playoff. In 1984, Pete Rose returned to the club as player-manager under new owner Marge Schott. Though Schott's business practices were sometimes highly questionable, she appeared to be the Reds number-one fan, sitting in the stands and greeting those sitting around her. Rose's popularity also continued to climb, as he broke Ty Cobb's hitting record. He led the team to four second-place division finishes before MLB banned him for gambling, a ban that still stands. Lou Piniella replaced Rose, and in 1990 the Reds held first place from opening day to the end of the season, becoming the first team to achieve this in a 162-game season. The Reds won the World Series that year by sweeping the A's.

Though they haven't come close to equaling that success since, they did manage to win the NL Central in 1995, with shortstop Barry Larkin winning the MVP award that year. In 1999, they won ninety-six games with a very young team, though they lost to the Mets in a one-game playoff for the wild card. In 2000, Ken Griffey Jr., widely considered the best player in the world at the time, was traded to the Reds. The trade brought back a hometown kid and turned the attention of the world back to Cincinnati. Since the trade, Griffey's health has not held up and many have called his place in history into question. His less-than-promising start as part of the Cincinnati franchise has disappointed and frustrated many fans, while his contract has handcuffed management.

On the final day at Riverfront, the fans didn't seem disappointed. It is possible that they had become resigned to losing at Riverfront but were still full of hope that the new stadium would kick start another winning era. Those present were the truly loyal fans, not the group I would have encountered during a typical day at the park. We were all in Cincinnati to celebrate baseball and what it meant to us. Following the game, the Reds brought back players from the previous thirty years. Many were names that I had long since forgotten, such as Ed Armbrister, Clay Carroll, and Rawley Eastwick. Others were all-time favorites, including Paul O'Neill, Joe Oliver, Dave Concepcion, and other members of the Big Red Machine. Only Seaver and Morgan were missing, both because of broadcasting duties elsewhere—and, of course, Pete Rose was absent. We had wanted Pete to appear, and many likenesses hung from the stands on banners, but the only number 14 to make an appearance was the one painted on the pitching mound by a renegade Tom Browning. Rose wasn't only in the fans' thoughts that night. Players from Larkin to O'Neil to Cesar Geronimo recounted stories of Pete when asked about their favorite memories at Riverfront. It wasn't that we didn't see what Pete had done as wrong, but we wanted to honor him all the same for the joy he had brought us as he hustled down the line. It's a feeling that has not yet been equaled in Reds' history.

9

Winning the Game

I had worked in theater for almost twelve years, and at the Juilliard School for nearly seven, when I decided that I needed to do something different with my life. I wasn't sure exactly where I was going, but my decision to visit each stadium in the league led to a lot of other good ideas. My job at Juilliard, managing the lighting and sound department, didn't give me the best credentials to move on to another field, but as someone who had watched theater for years, I understood how a play, a dance piece, or a musical composition could take the audience on an emotional journey. I also knew that the point of the performing arts was to perform for the audience—they are essential to the success of the performer.

I wasn't sure how I was going to express this idea to anyone outside of the live performance arena, and I wasn't even sure how it related to sports in particular. Television people seemed interested in my ideas, but without the practical knowledge of how to turn them into reality, my presentations went nowhere. However, when I began contacting teams about writing a book about the fans' experience, I received some interesting responses. Some teams were very generous and answered my questions, while others didn't seem to want to give me the time of day. The Atlanta Braves, the first team to respond to my initial request for information, were generous with their time, even though they couldn't fully accommodate my needs. As a successful team with plenty of media resources, however, their willingness to help encouraged me to undertake my adventure.

I soon began to discover that getting what you want from a professional sports team depends on how much you believe in your goal. (Well, being reasonable with your requests also helps.) When they saw my enthusiasm, people *wanted* to help me, and as I went from stadium to stadium, I met players, agents, coaches, reporters, and front-office officials that were willing to do what they could to answer questions and track down information for me. I underwent a constant learning process about teams, departments, and the protocols of dealing with each. As the game has evolved, it has become so complicated, both on and off the field, that no one who isn't fully immersed in the profession could hope to understand it. As I tried to do just that, I quickly came to understand why the gulf between professionals and spectators exists.

I attended ninety-five Major League Baseball games in one season, as well as quite a few minor-league ones, and my knowledge of the game and of the business grew exponentially. As each series progressed, I could usually determine the "big picture" from the manager's perspective as far as the action on the field was concerned, but in two days it was impossible to learn everything about what went into assembling a team and getting them ready to take the field. Baseball is a big industry, and as the number of people required to put on the "show" became clearer to me, I became ever more amazed at what a phenomenal feat this is.

I didn't go to as many games in 2003, spending more of my time doing the background research necessary to give a context to the notes I had jotted down in the ballparks. The Mets, my local team, were having their second horrible season in a row. Both in 2002 and 2003 they had made a splash in the off-season by signing marquee players. Some were aging former greats who had gone through rehabilitation, like Mo Vaughn, while others, like Tom Glavine, were certainly number-one guys at their position but may not have been the best fit for the Mets. Following the poor 2002 campaign, when the play on the field had become more than disheartening to the few people still attending games in September, the Mets raised ticket prices. Though Glavine was one of my favorite guys in the game, I felt that raising prices was insulting to the season ticket holders who had remained loyal though the previous year's debacle. Some gesture—and that's all one can really ask for—should have been made to the loyal folks who had supported the team for years. The Mets should have been grateful that season ticket holders were willing to return at all, and they should not have raised prices; perhaps even a discount was in order. I went to a few games early in the 2003 season, but I discovered that very little had changed. The team's All-Star players were playing at their worst, and I was actually relieved that I had chosen to protest the price increase by not renewing my subscription.

There were some teams I had greatly enjoyed watching in 2002, and I made sure to catch them as they swung through New York. These included the Angels, the Giants, and the Marlins. I watched the Reds on opening day in their new park, and again midway through the season. After that first game, against Pittsburgh, I was convinced they would lose ninety-five games that season. (They proved me wrong by losing only ninety-three.) The Cubs had made a number of moves in the off-season that promised to make 2003 a special year for them, so I went to several of their games at Shea as well.

As for the New York teams, the Yankees weren't playing as well as they had in recent history, and, as I noted, the Mets were simply abysmal, at least in the beginning. One by one, their aging, expensive veterans succumbed to injury, and the team began dipping into its promising minor-league resources. At first, the moves seemed desperate, but slowly I began to see a change in attitude on the field. These guys actually wanted to be there.

I always attend at least one Cardinals game each year as well. There is something about the storied National League club that fills me with glee. It might be the uniforms, or memories of Ozzie Smith doing back flips—I am not quite sure. The Cardinals were challenging in the NL Central Division despite a weak pitching staff, and Albert Pujols was always impressive to watch. I headed out to Shea torn about whom to root for. Usually a fan of the underdog, but with a fondness for Cardinal Nation, I sat waiting for one team to win me over, either with great play or with a show of enthusiasm on the field. The Cardinals took the lead early on that beautiful summer day, with Jae Seo giving up a home run to Pujols in the first and a single to Scott Rolen in the second. Rolen was moved over by a single from Tino Martinez and scored on sacrifices by Miguel Cairo and Mike Matheny. The Mets scored one run in the bottom of the third, but the top of the fourth saw the Redbirds score five runs off of two walks, a double, and two back-to-back home runs by rookie Bo Hart and J. D. Drew, putting them ahead 7-1. The Mets got a mini-rally going in the sixth with a single by Ty Wiggington and a home run by Tony Clark, but even those two runs were answered by the Cards in the seventh, when they scored three more, making it 10-3. The crowd of 30,000 started heading for the gates, thinking there was nothing more to see here. Early on I had been rooting for the Cards. I like Tino, I liked what I had heard about Bo Hart, and of course I was there to see Pujols hit that first-inning home run. The Mets, though, seemed to find a new spring in their step, and even Roger Cedeno seemed to be running hard and playing to win. They had had two 1-2-3 innings where no Cardinals batter reached base. In the eighth, the Mets scored one more run, off Josh Pearce, but Jose Reyes, the young phenom shortstop, grounded to short to strand two runners. The next wave of fans left. The top of the ninth was uneventful, except for an intentional walk to Eduardo Perez.

The bottom of the inning was the Mets' last chance, and I decided to stay until the end—there were only three outs to go, and as I had learned from my time in theater, one should never leave until the final curtain. Jason Isringhausen, the Cards' closer who had recently come off the disabled list, came in to start the inning. Vance Wilson was sent up to bat as the pinch hitter, and he reached first after the third strike dropped out of Matheny's glove and rolled away. He then moved to second on a wild pitch. Jason Phillips singled down the line and it looked like it would go foul, but the ball took a weird hop just inside the bag and stayed fair. Wilson scored and Phillips was on first. Phillips then moved to second, also on a wild pitch, and suddenly, with the score now 10-5 with a man on second and no one out, it seemed like anything could happen. Timo Perez flew out, and Ty Wigginton grounded to short. Tony Clark came to bat and singled to right, and Phillips scored, making it 10-6. Clark then moved to second on a third wild pitch. Next up was Joe McEwing, who bunted back to the pitcher, but with the third baseman anticipating the bunt and playing shallow, there was no one at third to receive the throw. There were now two outs with men at both corners.

Isringhausen was yanked, and Pedro Borbon came in to close the game. A bad bounce, three wild pitches, a dropped third strike had begun to make these Cardinals look a little like the Red Sox of 1986—a team full of bad luck. They were simply making mistakes, and the young Mets were capitalizing on each one. Raul Gonzalez was at bat, having taken over in left in the eighth. He doubled to left, scoring Clark and moving McEwing to third, making the score 10-7. The remaining fans were on their feet. Roger Cedeno came to the plate. He had already hit three singles today, but this season he'd batted poorly with runners in scoring position. I started biting my nails, repeating the mantra "You gotta believe, you gotta believe," over and over as my neighbors snickered at me for relying on Cedeno. Roger hit the ball to deep left center near the wall, where it fell between outfielders. Two more runs scored and Roger was on first: 10-9. The remaining fans roared with excitement. We imagined the fans who had left in the seventh getting home to find out about the 9th inning they had missed. Jose Reyes came to bat and singled, sending Cedeno to third base. In the stands, people were jumping up and down. We had batted through the side and Wilson was back at the plate. After each pitch, the crowds' chant of "Let's Go Mets" grew louder. We stomped our feet and clapped our hands. Finally, the windup came, and Wilson saw his pitch; he swung and hit a long fly ball to the left fielder to end the game. The Mets had lost.

I looked around and saw people smiling despite the loss. The Mets, as usual of late, hadn't won. But they hadn't given up despite seemingly incredible odds. These young guys seemed to believe against reason that they could beat the Cardinals, and they had gotten the fans on their feet, perhaps believing it too. The crowd had banded together to chant and clap and cheer—and they'd had something real to cheer about. Outside the stadium, as people made their way to the parking lot and subway station, joy was on everyone's face. In two years, I hadn't seen so many smiles at Shea, especially not after a game the team had lost.

The amazing late-inning rally was symbolic. This new team, the Mets' future, was full of fighters, and suddenly fans felt the dying franchise had a pulse. If they could come back in a game that didn't matter much, perhaps the team could come back from these two miserable years. Hope had been restored at Shea, as it had so often been before. The players on both teams that day had taken the fans on an emotional journey, one they weren't expecting. The difference between what happens in a theater and at a stadium is that in a theater the actors know roughly where the journey is headed and how it will end. Baseball players can envision how they *want* the arc to play out, but no one knows whether the audience will leave disappointed, enthused, demoralized, or exalted. On a good day, like this one, the fans will leave eager for the next game, and that is the best one can hope for.

Baseball fans throughout the summer of 2002 spoke to me about their favorite memories, connecting them both with family and with feats of athletic prowess. What they conveyed most often was elation and joy, though I did hear of the occasional heartbreak. One couple that I spoke with in Texas had just lost their young son to a rare disease. He had been a huge baseball fan, and even after he was no longer able to communicate verbally, he insisted that the Rangers game be put on the TV. The family had come to the park in the past, and A-Rod had spent time with him, autographing balls and taking pictures with the boy. This was the first game they had come to following their son's passing. The boy's mother had tears in her eyes as she talked about her son's love of baseball, and how sad he was when he was no longer able to go to the games. The Rangers had been very generous, facilitating his attendance for as long as possible. When she could no longer speak, her husband took her hand and told me that baseball had been a constant for them, something that was always there and would always be there, something that connected them to their son. Baseball, with its very long season, is always there. It changes and it frustrates, but it doesn't go away. It's something that everyone can rely on.

That's part of the problem. Teams may not understand why baseball is important to so many, but they know that it is. Just like players and owners, who said the fans would come back even if there was a work stoppage in 2002, I came to realize this is true. Whether it's the legacy of Babe Ruth, the magic created by Mark McGwire or the athleticism of Barry Bonds that draws us back, we want to be a part of baseball, just as we want to be a part of our community. We want to share in history and connect to those special moments. For many, their relationship to their team becomes part of their self-image. A Yankee fan who had suffered through the 1980s and early 1990s confided that he had thought about switching his allegiance to the Mets many times, as their blue-collar reputation was more suited to his own lifestyle. He had never been able to do it, though, because he valued loyalty above other things and felt that his ability to be loyal to his baseball team somehow reflected favorably on him as a person.

Baseball allows us to express emotions that we may not be comfortable expressing at other times. We can cheer and weep for our team when we really want to cheer or weep for ourselves. We can reach out to one another and connect over our team, even when we don't know how to reach out to others in other circumstances. We can create camaraderie where it hasn't existed before, as the 1968 Detroit Tigers did, bridging a racial gulf. Howard Rock, writing to *The Sporting News* in April 1970 regarding rumors that his beloved Indians might be relocated to Texas, said, "We are all what the past, our experiences—our defeats and triumphs—have made us. These moments of emotion help give us our very identity. Thus, an institution like the Indians is a part of our very being in the same way that school and family and religion have shaped us."[18]

What do we need from our baseball team? We need something to believe in. It can be a team or a player, and one could even argue that consistency is what we need, be it winning or losing. Though we are much more aware of the business of baseball nowadays, and are more affected by it as fans, we still want to think of those guys that play a game as being as innocent as our own kids, or ourselves when we could play. We want them to say please and thank you when speaking to our children, as we would want our children to speak to them. We want to think that they would do anything for the next guy, just as we like to believe that about ourselves.

We want to believe that anyone can win, because we want to know that we too have a chance. Along with that, we want to believe that our success comes from our own doing, and haven't been bought and paid for. Fans in other cities view the Yankees as a team full of hired guns, while local fans point to Derek Jeter, Bernie Williams, and Mariano Rivera, guys who came up through the organization. We want to feel that our team has earned its success. Now that we are learning to understand ownership's role, we want to know that they want what we want.

The new stadiums started a trend, attempting to turn back time and remind us of the days when we were less concerned with famous people's personal lives. The owners built stadiums that created the sense that things haven't changed that much. However, the experience the fan has in those stadiums has changed a lot.

As the gate receipts became less important due to increasing television revenue, the fans ceased to be as important. What owners now need to do is balance the needs of the fans in the stadium with their need to make money. Make us comfortable and happy and we will return again and again and be happy about it. Baseball can provide an escape back through time, a way to find peacefulness inside ourselves when our daily routines are packed with activity. The length of the game isn't really the problem; it's teaching us how to fill that quiet time again, with conversation and not commercials. Let the fan at home suffer through all the ads you want, but let those at the ballpark have a different experience, a relaxing and peaceful one.

Baseball players, even though they make huge salaries, can still capture our imagination and make us want to root for them, and they need to understand that should be one of their goals as players. Are we necessary for the game to be played? No. But it is our love of our teams that allows everyone in the business to make money. Fans need to become part of the equation again. If nurtured, we can mean something to the members of the teams, and to the advertisers footing the bill. Let us bring our kids often and give them lifelong memories, and they too will become patrons of the stadiums and the sponsors. One general manger told me that there are no baseball decisions anymore; there are only money decisions. I am asking that those money decisions be made with us in mind.

Give us someone to believe in and root for, and demonstrate that the club values him as much as the fans do. Also, players must value us, and if they want to be a part of a winner, then they need to make themselves available for community events. For our part, we will remain loyal, try to support the team's decisions and make our voices be heard when we need to. We will respect you and the game by educating ourselves about it. And we promise to work harder at letting you know what's important to us, besides an autograph. If we aren't coming, we are telling you something, and it's not that we want you to find another city. The definition of a winning franchise needs to expand to include welcoming, appreciative, knowledgeable and enthusiastic fans. And that can happen even if the team hasn't come together completely on the field. Baseball is the sport of the common man, woman, and child, despite your fascination with luxury suites. Roger Kahn once wrote, "Baseball is for leisurely afternoons of summer and for unchanging dreams." Make the fan's dream of enjoying those summer days come true and we, common men and women, will fill the stadium and help you build a winning franchise.

Notes

Chapter I

1. Warren Goldstein, *Playing for Keeps* (Ithaca: Cornell University Press, 1991), 108–109.

2. John Heyda, "Voice of the Fan," The *Sporting News*, 3 July 1965.

3. Goldstein, *Playing for Keeps*, 81.

4. Milton Most, "Fan's Point of View," *The Sporting News*, 30 May 1940.

5. Mike Lupica, *Mad as Hell* (New York: G. P. Putnam's Sons, 1996), 189–191.

Chapter II

6. Andrew Zimbalist, *May the Best Team Win* (Washington D.C.: The Brookings Institution: 2003), 22.

7. Murray Chass, "Rolling towards May Minus Three Mangers," *New York Times*, 28 April 2002.

Chapter III

8. George Vecesy, "A Whiff of Failure Is Still in the Air," *New York Times*, 31 August 2002.

9. "Baseball Log," *Pittsburgh Post-Gazette*, 7 September 2002.

10. Dick Young, "Enough Pouting and Pleas: Fans Eager to See Baseball," *The Sporting News*, 12 April 1969.

Chapter IV

11. Zimbalist, *Baseball and Billions*, 140.

Chapter V

12. Jerold J. Duquette, *Regulating the National Pastime* (Westport: Praeger Publisher, 1999), 8–22.

13. Ibid

14. Zimbalist, *Best Team*, 22.

Chapter VI

15. "Baseball's Most Important Product," *The Sporting News*, 3 May 1969.

16. Jules Tygiel, *Past Time: Baseball as History* (New York: Oxford University Press, 2000), 172.

Chapter VII

17. Leonard Katz, "With Spring Come Baseball Superfans," *Family Weekly*, 27 March 1977.

Chapter IX

18. Howard Rock, "Tribe Love Letter: From the Heart of a Fan," *The Sporting News*, 6 April 1970.

0-595-66950-6

Printed in the United States
35989LVS00005B/4